Dear Old Man

DEAR OLD MAN

Letters to Myself
On Growing Old

by Charles Wells

BACKBONE
PRESS
Nashville

Published by
Backbone Press
P. O. Box 58153
Nashville, Tennessee 37205-8153

ISBN 0-9646112-0-1
Library of Congress Catalog Card Number: 95-68181

Printed in the United States of America

For

Ann

Wyatt, Harwell, and Ann

who give me purpose for

the years ahead

Acknowledgments

Harvie Branscomb and Marc Hollender read portions of the earliest written manuscript and made many helpful suggestions. John Poindexter was a meticulous editor for the first version of the manuscript as was Ann Wells for the later versions, but neither of them bear responsibility for its content or style.

Throughout, Dotsy Brittingham has provided constant and strong encouragement. Without her enthusiasm, my will might well have faltered. Florence Davis, Britton Nielsen, and Ellen Hudson have been unflagging supporters to whom I owe much. My thanks go to Gary Gore, who deserves full credit for the book's handsome design, and to publisher Ann Wells, who has seen the entire project to completion.

I have used real names for those mentioned in a favorable light. For those referred to less kindly, or for others spoken of in times of their distress, I have not only changed their names but have also disguised their identities in other ways, so that I trust they could not recognize themselves should they happen to be among my readers.

My thanks go also to friends who have heard a few of the letters and have asked to have access to more, and to those who have expressed interest in this book and who have spurred me on to finish it. Having spent several years writing these letters, and many months more in moving toward their publication, I am grateful to all those who assisted me in the process.

❧ Contents

Preface

In only a few days, I will be sixty, an age that for many students of the subject marks the beginning of old age. I do not relish growing old, though I admit the alternative has even less appeal. Indeed, I fear growing old. It is not just that I fear death, for certainly I do. No, as fearsome as death appears, what can befall me in the meantime frightens me more.

For some years now, in my work as a geriatric psychiatrist, I have been privileged to come into intimate contact with many elderly persons, including my patients, and with their families and friends. Usually the initial contact has been in situations of crisis, but often the relationship has lasted and deepened. I have been spared little of the suffering endured by the elderly. What I have seen and heard and touched convinces me that only a few of us grow old with grace and dignity. What I have learned convinces me that old age is, without question, the most difficult and challenging of life's stages of development and growth.

We not infrequently hear of someone who is said to be growing old gracefully. If we listen carefully, however, we realize that the fortunate person, whether seventy or ninety, is not countering the forces of age, but is continuing to act like a much younger person. Having been blessed with good health and exemplary genes, he or she, despite the accruing years, is merely living and functioning much as always.

This is not what I mean when I write of growing old gracefully. As we age, most of us encounter physical and mental limitations, and as we do, we meet problems we have never faced before – major problems to be solved, often with reduced capacities. They present, I believe, a terrifying *terra incognita,* with no instructions to direct us. In America, "how to" books can be found for virtually every human activity, from babyhood through adolescence and beyond, but we have almost no guidebooks for old age. Having dealt with the vicissitudes of earlier life, successfully or not, the elderly are deemed ready to chart the wilderness of old age alone and without direction. To my mind, few manage to keep their objectives in sight, much less pass through without getting lost.

Too often I have seen the elderly destroying their reputations and their relationships because they have not planned for change, have not considered that new responses might be required by the new problems posed by aging. In order to forestall some inevitable problems, while I am still, I trust, of sound mind, I have written myself a series of letters telling me how to act, how to change as I grow old. I am sending copies of these letters to my wife, Ann, to my sons, Wyatt and Harwell, and to my daughter, Ann, with the demand that, in the years to come, whenever they observe me not following my advice (now so freely given), they pointedly insist that I live up to my stated admonitions.

Telling me how to behave will not be easy for my family. I probably won't take their instruction easily, even if they are reflecting my own words back to me. Doubtless I will grow testy and become defensive if they find fault with me – perhaps especially since I am acknowledged to be something of an authority on aging. Even so, I charge them to press on despite my ill humor and apparent lack of gratitude. Let us hope we can all manage to find some humor in my being called to task by my own words, written, I hope, with some wisdom aforethought.

Although I have written these letters as a guide to myself, they have also reached a wider audience, for I have read selections to Nashville's Centennial Club and Coffee House Club, to church groups, and at a few professional meetings. My listeners have responded to tales of old folks, such as Ellen Wemyss, still an enthusiastic doer in her 90's; or Uncle Alden, who, at age 84, insisted on hosting his grandson's rehearsal dinner in his home; to the numerous men and women who dance through old age with nimble feet; and to my own story of my dear little dog, Ramona. Those same listeners have welcomed my admonitions to heed the hazards of increasing age, to keep in touch with the world, to learn to say less and to listen more, and to learn to walk gently. Some have enthusiastically endorsed my statement that "Your children don't owe you anything." The most resounding response I have yet received came from an old gentleman in Kib and George Huddleston's Sunday School class. Though he appeared almost somnolent throughout my thirty-minute reading, at the end he jumped to his feet, and said, "That's just what I think!"

In their own ways, many of the people who have heard

parts of these letters have indicated that they, too, find my advice to be just what they think. They have encouraged me to speak to a wider audience through my written words. This I do now, in presenting to the reader my reflections, and my letters, ostensibly to myself, but really to all who would like to grow old with grace and dignity.

CHARLES WELLS

Dear Old Man

ᕱ *Learn to Walk Gently*

Dear Old Man,

Perhaps the advice quoted most often to the person growing old comes from Dylan Thomas: "Do not go gentle into that good night,/ Old age should burn and rave at close of day;/ Rage, rage against the dying of the light." These are the words of a Romantic poet writing to his father whom he perceived as old, whatever his age may have been. With a poet's intuition, he caught a truth that many deny or ignore – that in old age, passions may burn just as brightly and painfully as in youth. In his own life however, Thomas did not know how to deal maturely with those passions. He gave his father bad advice, which you must not follow.

William Butler Yeats made the same mistake in advising: "Grant me an old man's frenzy, Myself I must remake/ Till I am Timon and Lear/ Or that William Blake/ Who beat upon the wall/ Till truth obeyed his call." I have not sought further admonitions from poets.

Old age is not a time to rave and rage (if ever there is such a time in life), though many are the old who do. Indeed, rage becomes an everyday companion to many of the elderly, and it is a pitiable sight. Those who storm and bluster about do not reveal their strengths, but instead betray their limitations, their lack of self control, their need to intimidate. Their actions become senseless and embarrassing, embarrassing more to others than to the person involved.

You must learn to walk gently through that twilight. One secret of successful aging is gentleness. "Gentle" is a treacherous word, meaning different things to different people in different contexts. It may carry the feel of softness, or it may hint of diffidence and hesitancy, reflecting a sense of inadequacy, presenting a caricature of a gentleman who is kindly, but incapable of handling life's problems and complexities.

That is not what I intend when I tell you to be gentle. I do not suggest that you become a doddering figure unable to speak up, take a stand, or make decisions. I mean that in old age it is more important than in earlier years that you behave with restraint, with dignity, with good manners. This is even more necessary in dealing with family than with people outside, yet in my practice I constantly see people who act warmly and kindly to everyone except their spouse and children.

Good manners are the outward signs of a civilized society. Too often they are discarded in old age; too often old people behave as if, by virtue of age alone, they have attained the right to abandon habits gained in earlier life. You must learn and never forget that old age brings with it almost no privileges, only new responsibilities. Indeed, perhaps you should embroider those words in one of your unending needlepoint projects, and put it on the wall of your dressing room, so that you will be reminded anew each morning: *"Old age brings with it almost no privileges, only new responsibilities."*

I can almost hear what my daughter and sons will say if they read this letter: "Dad, come off it. You've always placed too much value on outward appearances; you've always paid more attention to form than to substance. You know that 'gentleness' business is only window dressing." Their criticisms are usually just, but not this time.

I want to explain why I put so much emphasis on gentleness of behavior in old age. One of the tenets of my work as a psychiatrist is that we become the persons we emulate. This doesn't mean that I believe we can become anything we choose, or that we can do anything if we try hard enough. It does mean, though, that I believe that most humans have the capacity to grow, to become better than we are, and that most often the key to this growth is action. Thus I ask you to act gentler, not to put on a show, though that may be preferable to its alternatives, but because I want you to learn to be a truly gentle man in whatever time remains for you before your death. You must heed the words which an elderly friend, who had been a dominating character in earlier years, said to me: "The one object, the one good left for old age is to mellow those aspects of behavior one has neglected, to bring to fruition the values of a good life. We can and must learn to be more temperate, more courteous, more forgiving."

There is nothing more pitiable, more embarrassing, than an old man raving and raging against the inevitable consequences of growing old. I hope you will protect yourself from this perhaps ultimate indignity.

❧ *Old Man, Hold Your Tongue*

Dear Old Man,

Old man, hold your tongue! Garrulity is one of the cardinal sins of advanced age. It can be a sin at any age, of course, except in those skilled in the art of conversation, but in old age it is particularly distressing, perhaps because we are more reluctant to deal with an old person who dominates conversation than to deal with the young. We will more likely interrupt a garrulous contemporary than one of our elders. Several years ago, friends of ours drove an elderly gentleman friend to an art exhibition in Memphis and later said that he talked the entire trip without stopping. Although they found his stories entertaining, they also had stories to tell. Still, they were hesitant to interrupt him, as it seemed disrespectful. No matter how old any of us are, we still can hear our parents saying, "Don't interrupt Aunt Margaret when she's talking," even if Aunt Margaret badly needed interrupting.

You must remember too that, unless you are the host, it is no longer your responsibility (if it ever was) to ensure that there are no lulls in the conversation. Leading the conversation is one of many torches you should turn over to the younger generation. No matter how much you may want to take over or interject your ideas, wait until you are asked to speak. If that does not happen, swallow your words, and admit that they may not be vital to the flow of ideas anyway.

This is one of many ways in which you must learn to give up control as you grow old. If you do not do so willingly, it will be forced upon you, for you will find any audience for your words to have faded away.

Perhaps this will be easier if you understand why.

First of all, you probably don't have much to say that you haven't said before, in fact many times before. You must acknowledge that your favorite stories are seldom the favorites of anyone else, and your friends and family have heard them all too often already. Even if you are lucky enough to have a new audience, and that is hard to come by in old age, admit that the stories of others are often of more general interest than your own. You must accept the fact that you may be far more welcome as a listener than as a talker.

Second, you must acknowledge that not much worth telling to others now happens in your daily life. For a long time you have realized that you did many things in your youth not merely for the satisfaction of doing them, but instead, so that they might make good stories for you to tell. Only a few of the young are wise enough to act for the joy of the action alone, without also having an eye out for what a fine story it can become. If you are lucky, you may in old age learn to do things for the pleasure of doing, without the aim of gathering material to make you more attractive to others.

I don't mean that you must sit mute, listening meekly to what others are saying. Of course you must speak up whenever something you have done or read or thought adds a new dimension to the topic under discussion. But beware,

beware, whenever you get the urge to begin, "Let me tell you . . . ." about a recent event in your life, or "I want to tell you . . . ." about something you have just read. Learn to revel in reminiscing rather than in retelling. Although you hate to admit it, your world has constricted. The things that excite you now are not those that would have excited you when you were the ages of your children. Spare them your enthusiasms, and, if you can, make theirs your very own.

❧ *Time and Freedom*

Dear Old Man,

Retirement, when it comes to you, will open up broad expanses of time in your daily life. You must make sure that you do not simply wander through these expanses and find yourself eventually in some dry and dusty wasteland of life, where you never intended to be. To paraphrase Lord Acton, "Freedom corrupts. Absolute freedom corrupts absolutely." Freedom offers opportunities only to those who are well disciplined.

You have always said that you don't know how people manage without a definite daily schedule. This schedule will be even more important in old age than when you were younger. Beware of regarding schedules, time commitments, and other routines as burdens to be dropped when you are relieved of the responsibilities of your professional life. They have always been your friends, and you must keep their friendship to the end, for they provide the framework that holds your life together. You have never handled leisure time well, and it's almost certain that you'll handle it even less well as you grow older. I'm not saying that you should have no leisure, but that you must see that it is fitted into your schedule.

Routines, rather than tying us down, can free us from mundane decisions and choices, providing time and energy for better things. I used to puzzle over the prayer recited each Sunday to the God "whose service is perfect freedom."

Isn't submission in service slavery rather than freedom? It took me a long time to learn that submission to the "tyranny" of a schedule liberates rather than enslaves. I cannot imagine a heavier burden than to wake each morning to face the question, "What do I want to do today?" or even worse, "What do I feel like doing today?" I suspect that, most of the time, I would spend half the day in indolent indecision, trying to come to the *right* choice. It will be so easy to let this happen to you. Don't!

You must also avoid substituting a daily list of "things to do" for a schedule of daily activities apportioned by the hours. It's tempting to try to impose order on your life by writing down the things you would like to do, listing them in order of importance, and then going down the list each day, accomplishing those things you've put at the top. The danger in this approach is, of course, that tasks expand to fill whatever time is available, especially if you have any perfectionistic tendencies (as you certainly do). You must ration the time you will spend on each endeavor, else you will never get to the bottom of your list.

Recently I heard a patient, herself nearing retirement, speak disparagingly about a gentleman who had retired some years before. "He has to get in his golf game every day," she said, annoyed because it had kept him from doing something else she wished him to do. She went on, though, to talk of how busy he was and of the many things he got done. I thought silently, "What a smart man! He's got his schedule worked out, and he sticks to it."

Clearly *you* must schedule your life in retirement as tightly as you always have and be just as rigorous in keeping to your schedule. There must be a time to rise and a time to lie down, a time for exercise and a time for tending to finances, a time for household chores, and a time for community and church responsibilities. But within this schedule you can also breathe a new freedom that you haven't experienced since your teens – a time for writing, a time for reading, a time for gardening, a time for needle-point (I hope by then doing projects for your children's homes), a time for truly listening to music, a time for prac-ticing an active social life, a time for giving of yourself to others, a time for thinking, a time for prayer, a time for paying undivided attention to Ann, and perhaps above all a time for contemplating the beauties of the earth that God has given us and thanking Him for it. But all these won-ders, or at least a good part of them, you'll never find time for, and will miss, unless you find a place for them on your schedule, where they belong. Then, live by your schedule.

❧ Slow Down, Slow Down

Dear Old Man,

If you're going to make the best of your old age, you're going to have to change some of your habits, and that's a challenge at any age. Although you've got many habits that qualify for change, I'm going to focus now on your constant hurrying, the bustling busyness that has filled your adult years.

In your work, you've filled every nook and cranny of the day (and part of the night) with things that must be done and done quickly and done today. You have been willing to let go only when everything is tidy and complete. This would be bad enough if true only for your work, but hurry and bustle have infiltrated every fragment of your life. You remember how, several years ago, you took off several weeks to vacation in the mountains, then came home to tell all who would listen that on vacation you had written half a book and read a large number of other books as well. And only yesterday, Ann remarked that you had done a full day's work in the garden in the space of an afternoon.

Now you must train yourself to slow down, in almost every aspect of your living, not just because age and nature require it, but because you've got to learn to enjoy what you do for the joy of doing, not just for the end result.

For you, gardening provides the perfect example. It offers just about everything – the joy of planning and design, the pleasure of watching seeds and plants develop into beautiful flowers, and, of course, healthy, vigorous physical activity for you in the doing. Each step provides an effort to be savored and enjoyed in all its aspects. So far, though, you've made of gardening little more than a job to be done, a task to be finished, as quickly, efficiently, and correctly as possible. Even as I write, I realize the absurdity of your approach, as though a garden could ever be finished.

You've got to slow down, to stop your senseless scurrying about, to learn to savor every single aspect of your garden activities. Take time in planning so that you enjoy every possibility before setting your course. Lose yourself in garden catalogs, filling hour after hour with sweet possibilities. Give yourself time to prepare the earth properly for the planting, and feed your plants gently, regularly, and carefully. Be ruthless in your pruning, but do not be quick to rush in and prune. Watch your plants as they grow and take delight in them; look to see all the shapes and all the shades of green. And finally, when the flowering comes, sit back and delight in it. And if the flowers should be lavish and prodigal, fill your house and those of your neighbors with the blossoms. Just as, every summer for several years, a patient brought you from her garden great pots of beautiful, fragrant roses which filled your office – one of the loveliest kindnesses you can remember.

It was no accident that one of God's first works on earth was His creation of the Garden of Eden. With luck, and following His example, you will still have the time and energy to create your own Garden of Eden. I want so much for you to become a little old man, a gardener, endlessly puttering, tinkering, and petting your plants there in the beauty you and the Lord have created together. Slow down, old man, slow down.

❧ *The Richness of Time*

Dear Old Man,

Your richest possession in old age will be time. This may at first strike you as dissonant since you know that the years ahead are fewer, by far, than those behind, but for many years now, you've had no time. In fact, your whole adult life has passed in a blur of hurry. You have pushed yourself to finish everything quickly so that you could move on to something else. Even your pleasures have been pressured. You have rushed through every book so that you could finish it and get on to the next. Reading poetry went by the wayside because it went too slowly. During a concert, you have moved your attention to the next piece on the program rather than listening to the one being played.

Now there is time to look rather than to just glance, time to listen rather than just hear, time to savor rather than just taste, time to relish and delight in whatever the present may bring. I'll remind you of the difference more graphically. You remember how we all smiled to each other about Mr. Grace. At every party, he would "work" the room, moving quickly and with a gracious phrase from one guest to another, never having time for more than a word or two with each, until he had greeted everyone there – and then he was ready to go. Everyone marveled at how he could "do" even a large party so quickly.

In contrast, you'll recall the last party the Wills gave at

their Warner Place home before moving to the country. It was summer, and the garden was as lush and colorful as Giverny. Tables, set outside, were spread with bright cloths. Candles sparkled in the dusk. We all looked our best. Mandy, who had come with Jack from Cincinnati just for the party, said, "I'm going to take time to sit here and look at every detail, so that I'll be able to always remember what the last party here was like."

In that statement, Mandy caught both aspects of the time you can have in your own old age – time to experience and time to remember. Now you can afford the time to read a book slowly, just for the beauty of the writing. Now you can recapture your love of poetry, can take time to read the poems slowly, sotto voce or even aloud. There will be time to sit quietly on the porch at Beersheba, to look at Tother Mountain for as long as you like. There will be time to remember, to recall the experiences you've lived, to live them once again, now with a leisure you never allowed yourself before. Remarkably enough, I think you'll find most of the memories to be good. Somehow time, and perhaps the grace of God, affects us so that most of the bad moves out of focus. We can hardly see it, whereas the good things from our past bubble to the surface clear and fresh to give us joy. And if Ann should, at such a moment, ask what you are doing, you'll reply, "Nothing." But if she should ask what you are thinking about, you'll surprise her with a happy vignette from the past.

That's why I've advised you to make time in your life for doing nothing. Your own personal videos of memories stored from the past won't appear on the screen if you keep too busy. Somehow you must let your mind wander and explore almost forgotten crevasses of the past, so that some of these treasures will come to light. Take time, old man, take time.

❧ Alone Together

Dear Old Man,

Since it appears certain that your daughter and sons will not live out their lives in Nashville, you and Ann must plan for an old age quite different from your friends who will have children and grandchildren close by. You will have each other, but nevertheless you will be alone together, and inevitably one of you will be truly alone. You must take practical steps to manage your lives effectively – and you must do so without feeling sorry for yourselves. Above all, you must not cause your children to feel guilty.

You must first accept that, although Nashville will always be home for you, it will not be for your children. The sense of home can be subtle, almost mystical. You recall that you never felt at home in Ashford, even though you spent the first twelve years of your life there. So I'm not sure you can do much to help your children establish their own sense of home wherever they may live, but you can try. You must begin by focusing on the places where your children live, where you must learn to be a guest. Your travels to visit them may come at a stage in life and often during holiday times when you would find it easier to stay in Nashville. If they should marry, you must learn to share them with their in-laws, and you must also foster their establishing holiday traditions in their own homes.

If you and Ann are to maintain yourselves securely without close family nearby, you must develop an alternative support network. You will need your friends even more, especially younger friends. And friends need cultivation, just as does a garden. You may require assistance with cleaning, cooking, maintenance, and perhaps driving. If your finances permit, you must pay well for these services. If not, then you must accept assistance from public agencies. You can utilize supports such as "Meals on Wheels," and organized safety networks such as Lifeline. Be sure that you continue your involvement in church activities and community organizations, for they too can fill voids in your life.

You must see to your own supporting networks not only for yourself but for the sake of your children, for they will surely worry about your living alone far from them. If they insist that you have household help, then accept it. You need only recall Mr. Carstairs to realize the trial you might become, for he insisted on living alone in his large apartment, even though he had frequent falls. When he finally agreed to a companion, he wouldn't pay a decent wage, and became angry when his daughter surreptitiously supplemented the wages he was willing to pay. On top of that, he drove away several companions with his constant criticisms. Yet Mr. Carstairs was, in other aspects of his life, a good person. Remembering his example, you must do all you can to reduce your children's anxiety about your growing into old age far from family support.

To do otherwise will foster worry in your children, perhaps guilt, and guilt is one thing you must never create in them. You have always prayed for your children to be independent, stretching their talents to the fullest, and you must be sure that your needs in old age in no way keep them from doing so. You may not be able to prevent their guilt, but you can make sure that you do not foster it. Remember, you can promote guilt by what you say as well as by what you do. If you think about it, almost any statement which you make could arouse guilt. For example, if you say, "It's good to see you; it's been such a long time," seemingly a joyous, factual statement, you can be heard to mean, "You've been away too long; you should have come home sooner." Or, "You know you're always welcome at home. We love to have you" can be interpreted as a reproach, suggesting that they do not visit enough. It may be that you can't avoid such interpretations, but you can take pains with your words, scrupulously avoiding those suggesting that you feel neglected because your children aren't living close by, able to help when you truly need them. Remember that, unless you are unwell, you can visit them as much as is wise for either them or you. Remember also, if you had insisted they live near you, that they might never have pursued their goals elsewhere. Indeed, they might have been miserably restrained by the chains of responsibilities which bound them to you and to Nashville.

When Wyatt was living in North Carolina, he provided a clear illustration of the very point which I am making. Having returned to Chapel Hill from several days of research in Washington, he wrote, "I've never been so glad to get back home." I thought to myself, Wyatt is at home in Chapel Hill. He's done what you always wanted for him. He's finally established a new home for himself.

❧ The Selfishness of Old Age

Dear Old Man,

You must constantly guard against reverting to the selfishness of childhood. Perhaps it has always been so, but I note increasingly in older people an assumption that they are special by virtue of their age alone – and thus like children should be cared for and allowed to have their way.

I don't automatically equate putting oneself first with selfishness. On the contrary, putting ourselves first is often a sign of healthy self-reliance and self-esteem. It is, if you like, a sign that we regard ourselves as valuable persons. Carried to the extreme, however, it becomes grasping and selfish.

Having seen this again and again in various guises in my work, I've come to realize how insidious and pernicious it can be. It appears in many ways – in the man who, upon retiring from a demanding job, assumes that his wife should devote all her efforts to making his life comfortable and effortless; or in the woman who insists that her children call or visit daily and who has her feelings hurt if they miss a single day.

This doesn't happen only to those who have been grasping and self-centered all their lives. It can happen as well in those who have been generous and giving, and most likely arises from the unconscious assumption that old age carries with it many perquisites. It also comes from the dictum that young people must respect their elders. But there is a clear, almost bizarre, exchange here. While less is required of the young person, in turn he or she has less freedom. In old age, however, less is required of the elderly, while at the same time they are free to do as they choose. Or so they think.

But I have attended to only one aspect of selfishness, and must address another, which is to be ungiving. While I admit that I have little evidence about this area of behavior in old age, I strongly suspect that most older people are less giving than are the young. There are some reasons for this, if we think of life in terms of accretion and depletion. During our younger years, we fill our storehouses as best we can against the winter of old age, when we expect to live on what we have stored – and if something is left over, we pass it on to the next generation.

Even if you are fortunate enough to fill your storehouse brimful, you will find it too easy to put all the emphasis on guarding it against depletion, forgetting to live on what you have reserved. You must protect yourself from this error, and you must continue to give as an essential element in your daily life. Giving doesn't necessarily involve money. You can give in many ways – in a volunteer job, in visiting regularly in a nursing home, by looking after a neighbor's child for a few hours, by telephoning regularly to a housebound friend. All these forms of giving will replenish rather than deplete your larder.

Once again, I put to you an impossible task, and I can understand your asking me irritably, "How am I supposed to keep giving when I don't know how much of what I've stored up I will need to keep Ann and me going till the end?" And, of course, I can't give you an answer. All I can say is that you must remember that giving is as essential to the complete life in old age as it was in youth. You must continue to give, no matter how near empty the larder may appear. I strongly suspect that he who gives most lives to the end most contented.

ᕤ *Asking for Special Favors*

Dear Old Man,

Let me continue with my admonitions about the dangers of selfishness in old age. For some years now the media has focused on the selfishness of the "yuppies" or baby boomers. It has labeled them the "me" generation, people seeking instant gratification, willing to spend all the money they make, even borrowing against the future to achieve satisfaction. While I cannot judge the accuracy of those accusations, I ask you to be equally critical of the older generation.

When you look dispassionately at our society today, I believe you will find no segment which has asked for or received so many special favors as have the elderly. And they still ask for more. People over sixty-five qualify for extra deductions on certain taxes. When they sell their homes at a profit, they receive special treatment in capital gains taxes. The Medicare system heavily subsidizes their medical care. They receive Social Security payments which are probably far greater than the contributions which they paid while working, and further, they pay only minimal income taxes on such payments. Property taxes are often reduced for the elderly. They receive discounts at cinemas, pharmacies, hotels and motels, and even through some insurance companies. To top it off, the AARP (American Association of Retired Persons), one of the most powerful lobbying groups in Washington, works constantly not only to maintain but also to expand these perquisites.

While this special treatment is fair in our democratic society, I must warn you of its long-term implications. Elderly persons receive dispensations solely by virtue of their age, or because they are disadvantaged (to use a current term, differently advantaged), or incapable of taking care of themselves, or are unable to pay their own way. Looking a little deeper, you will recognize that this denigrates the entire older group, and the individuals within that group. This may be the ultimate example of ageism, and it is fostered by the elderly themselves.

I do not deny that many old people need and thereby merit the support of society. On the other hand, many of them are reported to have more money for discretionary spending than ever before. Subsidies which have age for their sole determinants foster the public's prejudice about the old. I must conclude that aid for elderly persons should be based on their need, not on their age.

To take this one step further, should I ask you to refuse the established privileges of old age? I don't have the answer. For example, I cannot conceive the problems to be brought down on your head if you refused the tax dispensations granted to those over sixty-five. I suspect that the result would be endless correspondence with the tax authorities, who would have no protocol for dealing with such behavior. Symbolically, this morning I've torn up the gold card allowing me a reduction for the cinema because I am over fifty-five. Perhaps my act is little more than a gesture, but it makes the clear statement: "Don't give me special privileges just because of my age."

Surprisingly, my thinking along these lines has given me

an unexpected sympathy with elderly persons who refuse to admit their age. I had always viewed such behavior as a shameful attempt to preserve the illusion of youth. In this context, though, I begin to see it differently, almost as a plea not to be treated with condescension on the basis of years alone. I hope you will never stoop to such deception.

⨎ *The Less Said, the Better*

Dear Old Man,

You must learn to face the almost inevitable companions of old age, disease and illness, and to deal with them forthrightly and realistically. At the same time, you must not let them become the focus of your life. You must recognize that nobody, including those nearest to you, is much interested in your ailments. Though they may, despite all your efforts, become your consuming interest, they will never assume that importance for others. You should recognize that "How are you?" or "How are you feeling" are mere salutations, usually the equivalent of "Good day." Only on rare occasions should you treat them as a serious inquiry into your physical state.

How should you reply when such questions come from family and close friends who possibly have some genuine interest in how you feel? Of course, there's no problem if you genuinely feel well. But if you don't, there's the rub. You may be caught at such a moment longing to blurt out the truth. But here I give you a stern directive: the less said, the better. Even when you feel very unwell, it may be best to say simply, "This is a bad day. Let's talk about other things."

At the same time, I don't want you to think I'm advocating a basic secretiveness or dishonesty about your health or lack of it. If you develop serious illness, or disorders that may significantly affect the way you live, you should openly acknowledge them to your family and certain close friends, chiefly as a visible symbol of your honesty and openness with those you love. You must hide sickness no more than you hide success.

As an educational function, by talking of your medical problems, you are, in fact, teaching others how to treat you. For instance, if you have told your children about the painful arthritis in your knees, they won't continue to insist that you go hiking with them, or mutter to themselves about how inactive Dad has become. By an honest answer, you may actually divert attention away from, rather than toward, your health problem, just as you have done with your allergy to shrimp. Your hostess would much prefer to know of your allergy before dinner than to wonder why you are not eating your shrimp.

Whether your illness is a chronic annoyance, or a more serious threat to your life, you must attempt to put it aside, so that you can enter into the lives of others, and so that all human relationships can take center stage, so long as there is life.

❧ Be Careful

Dear Old Man,

You may consider alcohol to be a faithful old friend, a restorative balm, but as you age, you must school yourself to mistrust it. While you have always known that, despite its ability to relieve distress or induce a semblance of well-being, alcohol can be dangerous, you should realize that, as you age, its liabilities increase as do its attractions. Its dangers lie all around, brought on by interactions with our physical changes, as well as by the habits that come with a normal aging process. You may well need an elixir, but you must not turn to alcohol to find it.

Why is alcohol a danger? First, because the aging nervous system becomes quite sensitive to its effects. Thus, the second or third drink, which may have induced only a slight blunting of alertness when you were thirty, may pack a new wallop when you are seventy. So, unfortunately you may drink to excess simply by adhering to your former drinking habits. Second, many older people regularly take medicines, many of which enhance the brain's sensitivity to alcohol. Your doctor will probably alert you to the risks in these medicines, but it is your responsibility to bear them in mind.

In your world, though, the snares in everyday routine, especially in the retirement years, are far more insidious. You will have more time for a casual drink with your wife or with friends. You will have no more late evenings at the office. With your children no longer at home, you will not need a fixed hour for dinner. Your time for talking over a drink can begin earlier even as the hour for eating grows later. While you avoided weeknight social events during your working years, now you welcome them. Opportunities and temptations increase, and so must your wariness.

A truly abject sight is the older person who has drunk too much. When the young drink to excess, we may respond with a sly smile, seeing their action as a rite of passage. But we do not absolve the overindulgence of their elders. They should know better. At a large party last year, a gentleman quietly passed out at his table. Smartly dressed, chin on chest, arms drooping, he was there for all to see. And what could anyone say? You must remember this example, extreme though it may be. You must be wary, always alert to this daily domestic danger.

❧ Keeping in Touch with the World

Dear Old Man,

You've reached a stage in life where all of nature's forces are drawing veils around you. You can't see as well as you would like; you often can't hear all that is said; you can't move swiftly or surely as you once did. Taste and smell are all but gone. Barriers arise all around you. It will be very easy to let them cut you off from the world, to let them shrink the stage of your life to the few square meters of your home and neighborhood.

Narrowing your arc of vision isn't always bad, of course. Writers like E.B. White have always been able to look at the most familiar object or the smallest event and find meanings that enlarge their world. Unfortunately, most of us aren't E.B. White. Instead of recognizing trivia as insignificant to life, older persons often become preoccupied with the insignificant. Annoyances and irritations grow disproportionately, crowding out the rest.

Instead of dwelling on your own small irritations, you must keep yourself fully involved in life, as, for example, Ann's grandmother did, even when past 80. She kept in touch by searching the newspapers and listening on the telephone for every scrap of news concerning family, friends, or even acquaintances, and she wrote to them – letters of congratulation or of condolence, or notes just of interest. She also gave you another good example: she never turned down an invitation. Nothing was too trivial for her enjoyment, nothing too much trouble. A trip to the grocery, a ride to buy shoes for her great-grandchildren, a church meeting, certainly a party – she was enthusiastic and ready for them all. Another example comes from a woman once active in running her own business. Now over 85 and confined to her apartment, she called to congratulate Ann on her recent article in the *Tennessee Historical Quarterly*. She was keeping in touch, and she brightened Ann's day as well.

You must continue to study and learn, not just about the things that interest you, because you will do that anyway, but about the topics that captivate other people, especially the young. You will thereby renew in yourself the vocabulary of youth. Newspapers, magazines, television, radio – they will be your teachers, not only about the world of power and politics but also about books, movies, music, sports, drama, and style, all matters which interest and involve active people. You already have a good deal of practice in this area. For years you and Ann have been going to movies recommended by your children, often with enjoyment, but always so that you could talk with them about their enthusiasms. Remember when Wyatt called you at work to insist you and Ann go that very evening to see *Repo Man,* then at Hickory Hollow. And go you did, in such a hurry that you ate your supper – a sandwich – in the car on your way.

And you recall having lunch with the Friday lunch group of six gentlemen over 80, one over 90, who regularly invite a younger man to join them to discuss his work. I remind you too of Ann's Aunt Josephine, who, even when past 70, made it her business to be up to date on everything of interest to her younger friends. In response, she was often enthusiastic, sometimes critical and provocative, but always she had done her homework. She knew what she was talking about, and she drew the young in numbers to her side.

Another way to stay in touch is to keep yourself involved in important causes. Almost every truly vital older person I have known has been so involved – Philip Davidson in Alzheimer's Disease projects, Mary Ragland in the Opera Association, Ellen Wemyss in historic preservation. To the very end of his life, your father-in-law was active in the rehabiliation of prisoners, the care of the poor, and politics. Pick your causes with care. They must be important, concerning work that needs doing; they must include younger people; and they must involve you in hands-on activity. Trivial causes belittle you, devaluing your time and abilities; causes involving only the elderly keep you isolated and out of touch; sitting on boards which don't involve their members in the actual work of the organization does the same.

In summary, do not expect the world to keep in touch with you. You must keep in touch with the world.

❧ Dance!

Dear Old Man,

Keep up the dance! It's always surprised your friends and especially your colleagues at work that you love to dance. Somehow you don't look the type. You don't act the type. You're too buttoned-up, too inhibited, too much one who does everything by the book. It's surprised them even more that you are a good dancer. That probably comes more from a matter of practice than talent. Over the years you and Ann have spent far more time on the dance floor than have most of your friends, most of whom you've left sitting at the table and talking.

Dancing is one activity you and Ann can continue undiminished into old age. Perhaps you can even improve. In your sixties, you and she certainly dance better and enjoy it more than you did in your thirties. Recall the pleasure we had earlier this year when we joined a class in western line dancing. The group was fun, the dancing was new to us, and we even learned the "boot scootin' boogie." Now you have the chance to take those classes without feeling they're just one more commitment squeezed into a life already overflowing with work to be done.

You've been blessed with good examples by your older friends and the parents of your friends. Remember Delphine's mother, who you found yourself dancing with at a wedding party long ago. She was a tiny lady anyway, but on the dance floor she weighed absolutely nothing at all. And Mr. Cook, an indefatigable and accomplished dancer, became the loving object of each older lady's eye as he managed to dance with each of them in the course of an evening. You admired too the consideration he showed each partner, tailoring the complexity of his steps to each lady's dancing capabilities. You won't forget either how Dr. and Mrs. Burch always danced the night away together as though they were newlyweds, adapting their stately rhythm only slightly to each piece of music, whether frantic or measured, as they moved gracefully around the floor.

The champion of them all though was May Imrie. She was petite, quick moving, and graceful, and she remained that way all her life. She was a wonderful dancer. When the music began, it took command of her. She loved to dance, and her love was contagious. No one wanted to stay in his chair when music was playing and May Imrie was present. Her love of dancing and her gift for living sustained her through a long life and the death of three husbands. It was that love of dancing and of life that her three grandsons highlighted as they gave eulogies at her funeral. You will always remember that funeral because it was a celebration and a thanksgiving for her life.

So pray for abundant energy and nimble feet to follow you all the days of your life. How wonderful to be remembered as a happy old man, smiling and contented, moving with just a touch of grace across a crowded floor.

ᕗ *The Ultimate Loss of Freedom*

Dear Old Man,

No matter how kindly they are spoken, the words will hit you like a body blow (even though it's your pride that really is injured). Whether your wife, your children, your doctor, or all of them together, decree, "You really shouldn't drive any more," you must acquiesce. It is not a decision you can trust to yourself; you must trust the judgment of others.

To give up driving your car will represent to you, as it has to countless others, the ultimate loss of freedom. The driver's license has come to symbolize for all of us, in this automobile driven world, the freedom to do as we like, to come and go without asking for permission or assistance, ultimately to control our own lives. Remember when your children received their licenses at age 16 – they felt they had at last become adults. Driving represented freedom and independence for them, as it has for you, for so many years. Now you're being asked to give this up. And I'm telling you to surrender without a fight.

Why should you listen now to others and not rely on your own instincts? Among all the conflicts I've seen between older persons and those around them, none has been more rancorous than the one having to do with driving. In none has reason been so consistently on the side of family and friends and the lack of reason been so consistently on that of the older person. Except in cases when physical limitations have made driving clearly impossible, I've seen only a few instances when the elderly have voluntarily given up driving. I doubt that you'll be one of those rare people. Regrettably, but almost certainly, you'll have to be told.

In all my experience too, I've seldom encountered an instance in which the concern was not justified. No, the insistence of so many old men and women on continuing to drive, despite the counsel of others, is but another example of selfishness – an insistence on continuing to do what one wants, to put oneself first, despite the anguish, perhaps the outright danger, that it brings to others. You must not continue to put your own life and the lives of others into your no-longer-certain hands. It does not matter that there are other far more dangerous drivers still behind the wheel. You can take responsibility only for yourself, and you must do so even though it causes you much distress.

Aside from the physical danger to others, you must also consider financial prudence. Older drivers find it difficult to continue to maintain liability insurance, particularly if they may have been involved in "fender benders." Even if available, such insurance may be quite limited.

After you are no longer able to drive, you must not sit home and pout, thus constantly reproaching those who have imposed this on you. Indeed, this undeniable loss of independence need not reduce you to immobility. Though you can no longer drive yourself, you can find alternate transportation. If you live in a metropolitan area, taxis are available, and with a little investigation you may identify a special taxi driver who will accommodate your special needs. Even if you live in the country, you may find someone to drive you in his or her own automobile for a modest charge. I will even predict that the cost of taxis or a driver will be less than the cost of your own automobile, considering routine maintenance, gasoline, insurance, and depreciation. Though it's difficult, make a special effort to take pride in living cautiously and with due regard for yourself and others.

❧ *Your Rights*

Dear Old Man,

If you live long enough, you will almost certainly confront the harsh reality that you can no longer continue living independently without bringing distress to others. How far should you go to defend your rights to autonomy and self-determination when they impinge on the serenity of others? For the libertarian the answer is obvious. But for you, there is no simple answer.

I remind you of your patient Mrs. Bannister who, in addition to being 88 years old, suffered multiple fears that kept her from setting foot outside her own home, yet she insisted on living alone. She closed the door to both servants and nurses because they invaded her privacy. Even though she had a tottering gait, she would use neither cane nor walker for support. Her elderly brother, who lived nearby, kept her supplied with food and household supplies. Feeling compelled to telephone and visit daily to assure himself of her safety, he found himself constantly at her beck and call to arrange for the tasks required to maintain her house. In fact, he repeatedly neglected his own needs in order to sustain his sister in her fantasy of self-reliance.

I saw Mrs. Bannister again last week in the hospital where she was recuperating after breaking her hip and several ribs in a fall in her bathtub. She told me that she had no intention of moving, but wondered if she ought to start using a cane. "I can't stand having to be dependent on anything or anybody," she mused, ignoring as always the sustenance of her brother.

Another example is Mrs. Frankle who over the years has become unable to care for herself because of heart failure. As a younger woman, she welcomed servants into her home, but she now insists that she needs no help, that she is perfectly capable of looking after herself, even to doing her own cooking. Her daughter and son observe that she is giving less attention to her appearance and even to her personal cleanliness. She is steadily losing weight due to poor nutrition, yet she thwarts every effort they make to provide for her. Their lives are made even more difficult because every contact with one of their mother's friends begins with, "You've just got to do something about your mother."

These are near perfect examples that habits that serve well at one stage of life may become self-destructive at another. Self-reliance and independence, cornerstones of maturity and stability throughout most of our years, become stumbling blocks as we grow old and frail. The solution, which is not simple, demands a delicate balance between giving up and maintaining independence. Successful aging requires giving up a portion of control in order to retain some independence. Both Mrs. Bannister and Mrs. Frankle will, almost certainly, soon lose most of their freedom, not alone from necessity but because they have insisted on total control.

It's easy to analyze and understand such situations from a distance but much more difficult to see how you can keep them from happening to you. It's clearly not a one-time choice or decision. You must learn how to give up inch by inch, step by step, while at the same time holding on tenaciously to every bit of self-support that you still possess.

At the end of a recent party, we were standing, waiting for our car to be brought up, with two older friends and their much younger wives. Both men remain very active, decisive, and dominant. As their cars arrived, I observed each man slipping into the passenger seat while his wife got in the other side to drive them home. I suspect these men are aging successfully. Each knows his night vision is failing, and each has prudently given up driving at night. Each has relinquished an important talisman of independence while maintaining that core of personal independence which is the foundation of our selfhood. I hope you can do as well.

❧ Your Children Don't Owe You Anything

Dear Old Man,

Never forget that your children don't owe you anything. Without much question, the most important element in your life as an old man, except for keeping the love of your wife, will be your relationship with your children. The seeds for this have long been sown, and if not already firmly rooted, you probably can't do much now to make them grow. On the other hand, the mistakes that you make as an old man can break even the strongest ties. Relationships between parents and grown children break down most predictably when parents believe that their children should relate to them through duty rather than through love. Let me explain this more fully.

We are not far removed from the time when children were considered to be their parents' property, valuable commodities. Indeed, I have little doubt that my Grandfather and Grandmother Wells had so many children not because of total ignorance about birth control but because my grandfather knew that, without the help of children, he could never, as a part-time rural teacher and part-time farmer, work himself out of the poverty into which he had been born during Reconstruction days. And have children they did – eight – seven of them boys. I have no question they rejoiced in having boys, because they were thought to be stronger than girls and thus far more valuable working in the fields. After the third son was born, none of the children ever again had to work in the fields. Grandfather had succeeded. This in no way modified the basic rules under which the children were reared. They were ruled by their parents, with their first responsibility to do their parents' bidding. As the children grew older, Grandfather became less demanding, even as Grandmother became more so, possibly because she had only Carrie, the one daughter, to help her cook and wash and care for that family of ten. By the time I was growing up, my parents and I, along with all my Wells' uncles and aunts and cousins, spent every holiday with our Wells' grandparents, because Grandmother demanded it. Not only that, we all visited at their house for several hours every Sunday afternoon, at Grandmother's insistence. Although there certainly must have been love between my grandparents and their children, I never heard it mentioned, and there was never any suggestion that any of those acts were done out of love. They were ritualized over the years because Grandmother and Grandfather and their children, and even the children's spouses, jointly accepted them to be the duties of the children.

My parents brought me up very differently, in a more loving environment, and yet as I look back, the duty of child toward parent was emphasized just as strongly – yet it wasn't as obvious in so different a setting. My parents were by no means as demanding as my father's parents had been, and they gave me much more freedom to do as I wanted. Indeed, I was generally regarded as a spoiled only child because my parents gave me virtually everything I ever asked for. Unspoken however was the understanding that it was my duty to please them. And it was understood that the thing that would please them most would be for me to be perfect. If I did not please them, it was also understood that they might withhold their love. In a family in which love was valued, there was no doubt where my duty lay.

These are the origins of what some regard as my rather peculiar views about what is due between parents and children. In my work, I am often privy to the details of conflicts between parents and children, conflicts that often continue to the grave and beyond. My elderly patients frequently complain that their children, themselves often elderly as well, aren't doing what they ought to do for them, often coupling this with "after all I've done for them." What I hear in statements such as these is an unquestioned belief that parents who beget and raise a child have thereby a perpetual claim on that child. I simply cannot accept such a precept, and I continue to shock my patients when I respond that I don't think their children owe them anything.

Those who choose to have children have, to my mind, an unbreakable responsiblity to nurture them until they reach maturity. This is a totally one-sided contractual relationship, carved in stone before the child is born, entered into by the parents without the assent of the child. Parents must freely give that care, ideally in love, with the full understanding that the child has not pledged and does not owe anything in return. The parents are in debt to the child, not vice versa. The debt is owed until the child is mature, when both parents and child are set free.

How the debt is paid, whether lovingly or grudgingly, what the children are taught about the nature of the debt, and how the children assimilate and understand such sub-tleties determine how the relationship between parents and children will grow for the remainder of their lives.

Recently I've journeyed with a father and his three daughters through his long physical and mental decline, which left him totally demented. The daughters, them-selves nearing old age, wanted to care for their father at home. The only way possible was for them to stay with him. This they did, in rotating twenty-four-hour shifts, over a period of several years. In all my dealings with them, I never heard even a hint that they were caring for him for any reason other than their love for him. Their message was that they wanted to do this because their father was such a good man. It's no surprise that I also came to feel some of their love for him, along with a deep admiration for his daughters. Perhaps I've been especially caught up with this family because I know that if the father were in his right mind he'd never have allowed his daughters to make such sacrifices for him.

The central point I am making is that you must not expect your sons and daughter to do anything for you in your old age in repayment for what you did for them in childhood. You will doubtless need and want their help, but you can accept this help only if it springs from their love for you and their desire to live up to certain standards they set for themselves as sons and daughter. I hope you will be able to reject any help offered as a repayment for having bred and nurtured them.

❧ The Aura of Invalidism

Dear Old Man,

Almost certainly, by the time you need these letters, you will find yourself afflicted with one or more chronic ailments, perhaps painful, but without doubt distressing. It will be easy to use your infirmities as excuses, or even as justifications, for inactivity and isolation. They can become an addictive drug for you in old age, far easier to obtain than narcotics, and in their way just as dangerous, in part because they appear so harmless in the beginning just as all drugs do.

There will undoubtedly come the Sunday morning when you wake up feeling too tired to go to church, since your hiatal hernia was acting up and woke you during the night. Or your knees are aching today after all your work in the garden yesterday, so perhaps you might skip your exercises for today. Or you're tired – you've already had two evening meetings this week. Certainly others would understand if an old man called to say he didn't feel up to making tonight's Board meeting. It's easy to find excuses, and everyone is so understanding.

As with many aspects of old age, if you are to remain a first-class citizen, you must avoid the indulgences that will be foisted off on you by others. Certainly your fellow parishioners will excuse your absence from church, as will your fellow members your absence from the Board meeting. They will smile indulgently to themselves, for, "After all, Charles is getting up in years." You, however, must perceive their acceptance as dangerous and belittling, infantilizing – one of the subtler forms of ageism. And you have, in fact, provoked it, since the excuses you offer, digestive problems, arthritis, fatigue, are in fact shams – they are excuses you would not have dared use earlier in life.

This is a subtle distinction here. I'm not saying that you should make no changes in your daily life in response to the aging process or to sickness. On the contrary, I believe you should. Indeed, you have every right to choose to attend church less frequently, to exercise less often, or to go to fewer Board meetings. You may give up these activities because you no longer enjoy them, or because you prefer to work at other tasks, and you know that so little time remains for them all. But don't excuse your choices with illness unless you are truly incapacitated.

There is another message here as well. If you are ill, it's clearly more difficult to keep going, even when the illness isn't life-threatening. Should you be blessed with a long life though, you will need to push yourself. Otherwise you will certainly retreat into an isolated and sedentary life. That may not, in fact, be the greatest danger. The greatest danger is that with time your self-perception will then be altered, for if you persist in using illness as an excuse, you will surely begin to see yourself as sick, no longer truly whole, forced to curtail your activities. Not only will your self-esteem suffer, but if you fall into the habit of using illness as an excuse, you soon will be forced to prove to yourself that you really are sick and can't lead a full life. The aura of invalidism will slowly envelop you.

In very old age, the distress of chronic illness can walk with you like a shadow. You must carry it inside you and hope it attracts no more attention than does your true shadow. The alternative is to not walk at all.

ɘ You Must Continue to Live in the World

Dear Old Man,

I need to write you a coda to that last letter. If your wife becomes ill, you must not use her sickness as an excuse to withdraw from your daily rounds, any more than you do your own. Obviously, Ann is much younger than you are and, especially since she's a woman, can be expected to stay healthy for some time to come and to live years longer. Indeed, with any luck at all, she will long be at your side reminding you not to use your aches and pains as excuses. But beware if it's the other way around. I've seen people shrink from life and dry up, using their spouse's illness as their justification.

No, if Ann should become chronically ill, you must in fact be twice as active, being sure to take care of her while maintaining a full schedule of your own. You must realize that few illnesses require the total attention of a caretaker. Even in those that do, you can find helpers to assist in her care if you search hard enough for them. Your own personal services will never be indispensable. It's grandiose of you to think so.

You must keep active first and foremost for your own sake. Just think of your friend Wesley, who essentially gave up life some years ago when his wife became an invalid. For a few years, he continued working, going to his office part of every day, but then he abandoned that, and nothing else remained for him but seeing to her needs – even though they were wealthy and always had several attendants on hand. He had always been a vital, lively man, involved in the life of his friends and community, but now he's no more than a shadow of his former self, and when one sees him on his rare forays into the outside world he appears bent and shrunken. And what is there to talk with him about except his wife's condition? I suspect she may suffer terribly at the realization of how her illness has affected him, since I don't believe she was the sort who would ever have asked such a sacrifice of him.

The damage from such a turn in life is not limited to only husband and wife. You will recall another man who gave up everything to care for his wife, who had Alzheimer's Disease. He spurned help of every sort and seldom left her side, ostensibly because she did not want to be without him. He and she continued for years in a fantasy world in which he denied the severity of her losses. Harmless except to him, you might say, but you will recall as well his daughter's lament: "It's bad enough to have lost Mother to Alzheimer's Disease, but now we've lost Dad as well." And she spoke the truth, for even his children and six grandchildren had ceased to matter much. His obsessive devotion to his wife had become his only concern.

Withdrawal from the world to care for an ill spouse isn't good for the healthy spouse or for the children – and I suspect it's not good for the sick spouse. If Ann should be forced by illness to withdraw from the world, you must continue to live for her; you will be her eyes and ears in the world outside. Going out alone will not be easy – you've never been very good at that. You must come home to her though, filled with little stories and observations from the outside to cheer her. It's the sort of thing she's always done for you, bringing vignettes from her broader life to enrich yours, which has so often been fenced in by the long hours of your medical practice. If you devote yourself to it, now you can preserve and sustain, perhaps even infuse some joy, into both your lives.

❧ *Sunlight Is To Be Found There*

Dear Old Man,

I've dwelt so much on the problems and losses of old age, so much on its rigors and demands that it must appear cold and forbidding. That may be true but sunlight is also to be found there. I am writing now to tell you about those sunny spots of life in old age.

The most readily opened windows to sun and light are those of study and learning. No matter how feeble the body, those windows wait to be opened, even if perhaps your mind isn't as nimble as it once was. As I think over my own experiences with older persons who have been excited with learning, many memories unfold. The first is of a Russian emigre, Monsieur Porhoshnikov, who spoke to one of my college French classes at Emory many years ago. Having been reared in the Czarist court, he spoke beautiful and flawless French. Since Atlanta was not in those days populated with many people fluent in French, he sought conversation with students. On the specific visit that I recall, M. Porhoshnikov was concerned not with French but with Spanish. Though fluent in many languages, he had never studied Spanish, and as he told us in his heavily accented English: "I said to myself, 'Porhoshnikov, it's time you learned Spanish.' So a few weeks ago I sat down and began to study. It was difficult, and for days I thought, 'This is too hard for me. I'm too old to learn another language. I'll never learn Spanish.' But then after twelve days, it all became clear; it was simple and straightforward and easy; and I smiled to myself and said, 'Porhoshnikov, now you know Spanish.'"

Another example came to me recently from Ann. At H.G. Hill's grocery store she met an elderly friend, a lady now seldom seen because of illness, but on this occasion she was bright and vigorous – and talkative. "I'm having the most wonderful time learning to cook," she said. "I never learned how when I was young. Then I thought the kitchen was just the room you went through going to and from the back yard. But since I haven't been able to go out much, I've discovered what a wonderful place the kitchen can be. Now I'm always putting together something I've never tried before."

Closer to home are memories of Ann's mother, who took up painting after Ann's father retired, and took it up quite seriously. She was an amateur, but she was no dilettante. She studied with several teachers, worked long hours on her own, and became quite accomplished. Before her death, she presented several shows that were surprising for their quality and distinction. Her paintings still enrich our home and give us pleasure.

Beyond learning, there is fun to be had in old age. As I think back over my own life as an adult, many of the persons I've most enjoyed were elderly. First and foremost among them was my Aunt Annie, whom I loved from infancy "with a love that was more than a love." She was, quite simply, more fun to be with than anyone I've ever known, and she remained so even through her last and terrible illness. She was a great talker, with the uncanny ability to make every event in her life, no matter how trivial, fascinating. She always had a new story to tell of something wonderful that had happened to her. At the same time, she was anything but self-centered, and she was always intensely interested in what was happening to others. Especially to me. She always responded to my needs, whatever they might be. When I was at Emory, I needed a new white dinner jacket for our fraternity dance, as, at the last minute, I realized that my old one had become yellowed and shabby. Realizing that only Annie, probably not my parents, would buy one for me, I phoned her with my request. She sent me a handsome new white jacket the next day.

The list of older friends I associate with good humor and abundant living is long, and I can recall for you only a few. In my recollections, I never see Sarah and Pops Huger without smiles on their faces and their arms outstretched in welcome to their home, which they called "Club Huger," open at any time to their friends. To be in their home in Atlanta was to be enveloped in smiles and laughter and love. Pops is long dead, and Sarah now lives in a retirement apartment, but she was on the telephone to us within the hour last year when the bouquet we'd sent to celebrate her eighty-ninth birthday arrived. The roses were, of course, "the most beautiful I've ever seen," far more beautiful in her recounting than they could possibly have been in reality.

Jack Dewitt provides another kind of light-heartedness. He is cerebral, piercingly intelligent, at times acerbic in his humor, yet still warm and kindly.

To be with Harvie Branscomb is yet a different experience. My every conversation with him has begun, "Tell me now, Charles," followed by a question, often concerning my medical specialty. Usually I have had no answer to his far-from-simple questions, but they have always led to a lively exchange of ideas or information. Harvie always seeks to bridge his world to mine, or perhaps the other way around. Maybe that is the key to my joy in thinking of the five persons I've mentioned, for they have all sought to connect my world to theirs. They don't ask me to be a spectator of their world, nor do they play simple onlookers to mine. Somehow they have the magic to create a union.

You also recall that older people can be truly entertaining. Only a few weeks ago, Fred Russell presented to the Coffee House Club one of the funniest papers I have ever heard, as he regaled us with humorous stories culled from his lifetime as a sports writer. Afterward, urged on by members' questions, he kept us almost in tears as he extemporaneously told one story after another.

Also you remember Ellen Wemyss' ninetieth birthday party, which she gave for herself at Fairvue, her magnificent ante-bellum home. She was heard to express regret that there had been space enough for only seven hundred of her friends.

And finally, you'll smile when you think back on the series of costume balls which Gay Nielsen gave as she grew older. Doubtless the invitations evoked many groans of "Have I got to put together another costume," but no one wanted to be left out, and I suspect she received few refusals. Amazingly, as Gay grew older, the parties became even more fun. The last was pure joy, and Gay seemed the most joyous of all, though she was then too weak to dance the night away as she would have liked.

All these people have provided their own foundations for the happier corners of old age. Each one has emphasized giving rather than hoarding, which often dominates the lives of the elderly, and which leads to dry, colorless days. Hoarding should be for the middle years, when there is something to save for. Old age should be for giving and for generosity, both of which dominate the lives of my older friends. Through generous, giving lives, they have spread happiness around them.

❧ Sing No More

Dear Old Man,

Even now I'm too old to be still singing in our church choir and should have given it up years ago. By all rights, and by virtue of my age, I should have given up singing before people, even in a group, and should now be joining only the congregation in hymn singing. I justify my continued membership in the choir because I can still bring forth resonant, very low bass notes, and, after all, true low basses are hard to find. I know though that I'm singing on borrowed time, and I make every effort to sing softly except when those low notes come my way.

I'm not telling you this just to record the current state of my vocal capabilities. No, I'm writing because I fear that when you finally slow down to read these letters, however many years in the future it may be, you may still be singing in the choir, enjoying every moment of those wonderful Rachmaninoff pieces lovingly composed for low basses, and trying to conceal your faded high notes from the ears of your choirmaster. If you are still singing in the choir, stop! Resign this very minute! It may be too late for a graceful exit, so take your leave quietly and hope there are not too many sighs of relief at your departure.

In earlier years, you've been in choirs where singers sang on too long. You remember Melba Braquin. Although she had gracefully relinquished her position as soprano soloist after turning 50, she stayed on in the choir. Instead of gently blending into the chorus, she turned every high soprano passage into a solo, and she became a pariah in her own choir, because the choirmaster was too kind to ask her to leave. She had forgotten that church choirs exist to sing not for their own pleasure, but to the glory of God.

I have been thinking ahead for you, though, and see some ways for you to avoid giving up the choir, even when you quit singing. So many behind the scene tasks are required to keep any choir singing, and you could relieve the choirmaster and singers of many of those responsibilities. You can bring out and then put away the sheet music for practice and performance. You can type and copy choir schedules, and then you can see that the list of hymns and anthems for Sunday services is put into the Bulletin. You can contact missing members and recruit others. If the anthems for the week have been recorded, you might make a tape to listen to during practice so that members will know how other groups have interpreted the music.

Indeed, once you get started, there is no end to the list of ways you might be helpful, probably more than you would find time for. You can stay a valued asset to the choir, even without joining your voice with theirs, possibly far more valuable than when you sang. But if you are still singing when you read this, give it up, and do it now! The time has come for you to be quiet to the glory of God.

✑ The Joys of Giving (Up)

Dear Old Man,

You have often said that one joy of growing up is that you can put away not merely childish things, but also many other things that have come to clutter your life. I remember that wonderful spring afternoon when I gave up golf. I'd never been any good as a golfer, but most of my friends played, and it seemed sociable to join them. I worked to improve my golf, making countless trips to the driving range, or I'd rise at dawn just to have the course to myself before others arrived. But it was all to no avail. No matter how carefully I chose my foursomes, I usually had a score that could have bought joy only if the game were basketball. And so, on a memorable afternoon, after another disastrous round, I gave up golf, and almost at once I felt as though a weight had been lifted from me. I have never regretted it, even for a moment.

I'm reminded of an incident that occurred some years ago with a patient, a man from the country, old before his years, who had epilepsy. He was obviously poorly schooled, and so I was surprised when, in answer to my question as to how many years he'd gone to school, he answered, "Fourteen." He went on, "One day I was settin' on the steps outside the schoolhouse, and I said to myself, 'You ain't never learned nothin', and you ain't never gonna learn nothin', and I quit." How old were you, I asked. "Twenty-one," he replied. And what grade were you in, I continued.

"The second," was the sad answer. Fourteen years in the first and second grades. My golf was not much different.

I gave up other things in addition to golf, all things that I had enjoyed, but that had become a burden. First, I moved away from New York City, though it's still a good place for a short visit. Then reading the entire Sunday *New York Times* and the *New Yorker,* even though I still scan them from time to time. I gave up regular subscription tickets to the symphony, though find an occasional concert to be a joy.

This paring down, this putting aside pleasures which have become almost duties, cluttering your life, and leaving little time for the things that now matter most can be almost gratifying in itself. Take traveling – Old man, you don't ever have to be an organized sightseer again. I know that you will never stop going to distant places, but remember, it's enough just to go, be there, and enjoy. After our trip to France last fall, friends asked, "What did you and Ann do in Paris?" We replied that we had had no specific plans, but that we had walked miles through the city, and mainly, enjoyed being there. "Did you see all that has been done to the Louvre?" We had looked at it from the outside, but we didn't go in. "Was the weather good?" was the next question, to which we replied that it had rained every day, but still we had continued walking casually to see Paris on our own. "Did you go to any fine restaurants?" they next inquired. Indeed, we did, we said, but you may not have heard of them. We ate in some delightful small places in our neighborhood or in ones that JoAnn and Bill had told us about.

It was the best time we'd ever spent in Paris. And now I know it's all right to go to New York and not see a single show or museum, but instead to spend time visiting with Fletcher at home or walking with Ann through the city. It's all right to go to Washington and admit that you really don't want to see the Smithsonian. It's all right to go to Taos and not see the Pueblo again. When friends ask you to join them on a wonderful trip to Japan, it's all right to say that you'd rather stay a while in your cottage in Beersheba Springs. That's really where you want to be.

So take advantage of your age. Tell yourself that you really have no reason to do all those things that have grown unimportant to you. Take time to enjoy the new freedom of old age.

❧ The Seeds of Estrangement

Dear Old Man,

When you eventually retire, you will discover that the most treacherous quicksand of old age lies in the marital relationship. Indeed, damage can be done to even the best of marriages when the husband retires. This may sound sexist – as though only the husband has a job outside the home, as though only the husband, and not the wife, might retire. But that is virtually a fact of your generation and of your culture, and therein lies the basis for the problems that so often arise.

You must accept the fact that although you may retire, Ann will not. Although she may have been wise enough in her planning to take into account the likelihood that you might one day retire, she has almost certainly planned her life as a continuum. The activities to which she has devoted herself – her research, editing, and writing, her membership on a board or in a literary club – will go on. Although retirement will open up broad expanses of time in your life, it will do nothing of the sort for Ann. Indeed, most wives complain that they have less time *for* themselves and *to* themselves when their husbands retire than they have had since their children were young. You have spent most of your working life wishing you had more time to spend with Ann and your children, but in retirement you may quickly discover that they are now busy, and do not have a great deal of time for you.

As a cardinal rule, therefore, you must not expect your wife to make drastic changes in her life chiefly to accommodate your new leisure time. She has spent many years building her own daily life, largely apart from you. If she has been successful, and you hope that she has, her life will by now have achieved an internal order, a rhythm felt in her deepest self, an essential part of her being. Even if she appears to be willing, you must not ask her now to cut up the fabric of her life. Especially, you must not permit yourself to feel neglected because she doesn't.

To succeed in adjusting to retirement, you must make radical changes in your priorities and values. Throughout your adult life, work has claimed the largest share of your waking hours. In a real sense you have had little control over the number of hours that you worked each day. When you were not at work, you expected your wife to be available for activities with you. You will recall, I hope with continuing embarrassment, how miffed you once were because she demurred about leaving on a vacation on a certain day because she had a Board meeting then. Without thinking, you had assumed she should drop everything to join you. You must not carry such an attitude into the retirement years.

You heard recently of a woman who gave up her weekly bridge game because her husband, newly retired, expected her to spend the day with him. That seems too bad to me – from two standpoints. First, he should not have asked her to drop such an important ritual just to be with him. Second, she shouldn't have acquiesced. The implications are clear: his wants should carry greater weight than hers. It is always wrong to devalue the activities of another, but in retirement especially it becomes one of the seeds of estrangement, at a time when husbands and wives need each other more than ever before.

You must give Ann's habits, her activities, her responsibilities, value equal to yours, and you must not expect her to give up anything that she considers important just because you now have free time. Concentrate instead on the interests that you have always enjoyed together, and find time for them in ways that suit you both. Go to more movies. Occasionally try new restaurants. Check out that new store at a distant shopping center. Think about attending a concert at the Blair School of Music. You might even buy tickets to hear country music performers at Opryland, just as you did when you heard George Jones and Emmylou Harris. A world of common interests await you, if you both are careful to tread lightly in adjusting to your new free time.

❧ Space, Distance, and Old Age

Dear Old Man,

Throughout your years of marriage you and Ann have had not only your separate worlds of activities but separate worlds of space as well. Even if you plan carefully, your world of space will almost certainly constrict with retirement, and that constriction may lead to stresses in even the best of marriages. I'm defining space here as a defined area that we human beings tend to take over, to make our own. As a working professional, you have been assigned various areas called offices. You have taken each and transformed it into your own personal space, as have your colleagues. Even the secretary's desk or the student's carrel becomes personalized, visibly possessed by secretary or student, transformed into his or her own personal space. Your office now speaks of belonging to you, as it holds your prints of the West, an Indian rug, pictures of Ann, Wyatt, Harwell, and young Ann, of course your medical reference books, and even a stuffed animal or two to illustrate your occasional quixotic humor.

As your work week begins to shrink, you will need space of your own away from the office. While you may think you can find ample room at home, there are reasons to question this assumption. In most conventional homes, although space is assigned according to use, such as the kitchen for cooking, dining room for eating, and bedrooms for sleeping, space also tends to become the personal property of its occupants, as children may consider their bedrooms to belong to them, and the husband finds his work-shop or study to be his own possessions. A wife may think of the kitchen or dining room, or her home office, even the living room, as her domain. Understandably, she grows accustomed not only to using but to regarding the space as her own; while she may gladly share it evenings and week-ends, most of the time it is hers alone. While you have dreamed of having more time to spend at home, and Ann may have looked forward to having you there, if you are not careful, she may feel that your presence is invading her personal space. It is probably the rare wife who does not long occasionally to have the place all to herself again.

How can you deal with this problem? You have already made a start. Recognizing your need for a study of your own at home, Wyatt made the generous suggestion that you transform his bedroom into your study, since he was seldom there. With his agreement, you then moved out his beds, added a sofa bed for his visits, and moved in your desk. After buying a word processor for the room, you real-ized that you had made it your own. But where might you place the Nordic Track which provides the stimulus to keep your weight at reasonable levels? It has found a home in Ann's room, as she too has made her home elsewhere.

If you can afford it, I think you must also consider set-ting up a small office for yourself away from home, to become a place where you have relief from the telephone, a space for reading and for writing, perhaps for tending to financial matters. If the time comes when you are no longer seeing patients, you might rent a little office space from your partners. That arrangement would provide you and Ann not only with your own spaces, but, equally important, with some distance between you.

I suspect that married couples need to maintain some distance between themselves in old age. For most couples, this doesn't require any thought or consideration in earlier years; indeed, the demands of work automatically create separation, so that the challenge may be finding time for closeness, not for separation. In old age though, closeness, or too much of it, can be dangerous. It reminds me of what A.J. Liebling once wrote – that a gourmet must be neither too rich nor too poor. If too rich, he tends to eat recklessly and without discretion; if too poor, he can never afford to buy and taste the very best. The same may be said of closeness in the lives of most couples; too much tends to satiate, too little leaves emptiness and hunger.

For you, maintaining distance poses special problems because your principal diversions – gardening, cooking, reading, bargello needlepoint, writing – have been your activities done at home, and you have looked forward to having more time for them, such as time to perfect your little English garden which gives you and Ann such pleasure in spring and summer. You have always been a superb cook when time has permitted, and now you can prepare new pastas, or soups, or maybe even turn your hand to breadmaking. Almost every day you hear about a new author or a new book you'd like to read. Not to speak of your needlepoint, which now graces several chairs in your home, with others yet to come. And your writing – that may become the joyous avocation of your retirement.

Ann too cherishes her time at home – in her research into family correspondence, and in her study of Tennessee maps. She has even overflowed her own home office into

Harwell's room, where she houses most of her maps and her reference books. She has become increasingly fascinated with her computer, which has permitted her to write and to edit with ease. Although her interest in everyday cooking has diminished, she still relishes making bread, and spending time in the kitchen. So you both must be especially determined and ingenious if you're going to keep distance in your marriage when you're truly old and tied into your home.

What can you do to maintain that distance? Maybe you should return to school and study in the library there or in your outside office. You've always wanted to speak better French, and with our changing population, shouldn't you learn Spanish as well? You've had a special interest and talent in architecture and design, and could take courses in those areas. In college, you were a good bridge player. Has the time come for refresher courses and perhaps a venture into duplicate bridge? You could try tennis again. Or perhaps your friend Charlie would teach you lawn bowling. You could transfer some of your gardening activities to Cheekwood's botanical gardens which always need experienced volunteers. Since you no longer sing in the church choir, you might serve by becoming its secretary and music librarian. I'm excited about the prospects ahead for you, but you'll have to stay alert to make them happen.

Remember, in the early years of marriage, lack of togetherness causes most of the problems, while too much togetherness causes them later. With your and Ann's many lively and engaging interests, surely you can maintain the distance you both need, while finding new ways to enjoy your new time together.

❧ Sharing Household Tasks

Dear Old Man,

You must move cautiously in changing the ways in which you and Ann divide household tasks and responsibilities for the care of your joint property. For many years now, you've spent so much time working that she has assumed the major share of responsibility not only for household tasks but for home maintenance as well. You have done most of the work in the garden, really not work to you, but more a pleasure, as you have planted, pruned, started new seeds, and watched your garden grow. Even now, in your vacation retreat at Beersheba, you have started new gardens, planted bulbs, created edging around your driveway, thus spending happy hours.

Never a gardener herself, Ann has admired your work, photographed your specimen flowers, and done a little easy trimming. She has taken charge of household maintenance, summoning painters, plumbers, electricians, and window-washers as needed. You have always been a willing assistant or general in the kitchen, when time permitted. Ann and your children have savored the occasional meals you have prepared, even the long ago milkshakes for Sunday lunch, or your Sunday night omelettes. Because you will be devoting less time to your profession, it seems fair that you should take on more household responsibilities, whether they be waiting for the plumber or cooking supper. Besides, those are chores that you will likely enjoy.

You must remember, however, that you like to take

charge, and you must modify this as you and Ann work out reasonable assignments of responsibilities. One of the common complaints I hear from dissatisfied older wives is that, since retirement, their husbands have tried to take over the household. As one told me in exasperation the other day, "He's taken over everything. Why, yesterday I came in and found him doing the laundry, and I've always done the laundry." The other most common complaint I hear is, "He just sits home and does nothing, always expecting to be waited on." That, however, will not be one of your problems.

Part of your willingness to do more chores at home will arise not just from your sense of fairness but from your desire to continue to be useful. You must recognize though that every task Ann gives over to you may take something from her, perhaps her own sense of usefulness. At the same time, she must acknowledge that, if you assume more chores, you will then free her for her own writing. The most you should do is to offer to take over a portion of her domestic duties – if it is to her liking. Make the offer open-ended, try to refrain from making suggestions, and under no circumstances rush in to do things without asking. You two must first verbally reach an agreement, and then move on.

If she is willing to turn over certain tasks to you, and if you agree to accept them, then she has the right to set the standards of performance expected. For example, if she suggests that you clean up the kitchen each evening after dinner, she can expect you to do this promptly after the meal, and not wait until later in the evening, or the next morning, to wash the dishes. She also has the right to insist that you perform the task up to her standards. It's not enough for you to be slap-dash if she has always been meticulous. She also has the right to expect you to do the job regularly without being reminded each time.

On the other hand, she should not tell you exactly how to accomplish every step of the task, how to place each plate or glass or cup in the dishwasher, or how to sweep the kitchen floor. Too often I hear husbands who are frustrated because nothing they do in the home ever satisfies their wives. They then adopt, perhaps with some justification, a "what the hell!" attitude to the whole idea of sharing household tasks. And too often, I hear from wives that their husbands are "slow and clumsy" and useless in the kitchen. Perhaps they are forgetting the time years ago when they too may have been slow and clumsy and just learning.

In negotiating household jobs with Ann, you must be cautious about taking on too much, as in so doing, you may be avoiding building a broader life outside your home. How easy it will be for you to preoccupy yourself with cooking supper, working a bit in the garden, refinishing a piece of furniture, talking with the electrician, and then find yourself with no time or energy for other matters. You may fool yourself into thinking that you're making life easier for Ann, but instead she may be climbing the walls because of your constant puttering and tinkering. Be sure that you do not use your home responsibilities as an excuse to avoid the outside world which you need so badly. If you want to hold back the ever-limiting encroachments of old age, you and Ann must reasonably permit and encourage one another to be useful, both at home and in the wider world.

❧ Guardian of Ritual and Tradition

Dear Old Man,

As I think about old age, I become increasingly aware how few good roles in life there are for the old to play. Most of what I have written you about are minor supporting roles. They are concerned with holding on or keeping things together, not with serving any truly positive function, in the world or even in the life of your family. One role, though, belongs almost exclusively to the elderly, and it is one you especially will enjoy – that of guardian of ritual and tradition.

Ritual and tradition provide the cement of our society, but more importantly, they commemorate and celebrate, they give meaning to the most important things that happen to us in life – birth, christening, engagement, marriage, death. Indeed their involvement transforms each event into something more, makes it into a chapter in the family history, an event to be celebrated or mourned thereafter in yearly commemorations.

In my thoughts, I tend to make a distinction between rituals and traditions. The former I think of as the province of the church – christenings, marriages, funerals; the latter of the family – birthdays, anniversaries, holidays such as Thanksgiving, even parties such as our annual Christmas Eve celebrations. Even so, rituals and traditions are probably more similar than dissimilar. Although neither of these requires the attendance of the old, each needs their presence; and further, each requires the blessing of the old to be complete.

Our Christmas Eve family party, for example, needs Uncle Alden there to make it whole. On these occasions, I still feel the presence of Ann's parents, and Josephine and Rob and Jane who were often with us for these celebrations when they were living. Uncle Alden gives us continuity in a world of contemporaneity. My recent birthday provides another example. It was appropriately noted and celebrated by Ann and our children, but I was saddened to realize that only my Aunt Carrie remains to actually remember the day of my birth. All the others are dead. On such occasions the old serve not only by being there but also because they evoke memories of those who are absent and who are missed once again.

As I write, I ask myself whether anything more is required of you than your presence, and if not, why just the presence of the old man seems so important. I was about to write that certainly your presence must be benign, but that really isn't at all necessary. Aunt Josephine's presence was not always benign, because she often disguised her warm and giving spirit with sharp wit, yet we needed her with us.

Too, I'm reminded just now of a recent wedding reception when only a few of the generation older than I were there. It suddenly occurred to me that on that occasion, I was the older generation. I began to perceive that the presence of the old can become an almost priestly function. By their actions, they transform the event into something deeper and more meaningful. I remember the last year Jane was able to come to our Christmas Eve party, when we knew it would probably be her last. Her mind already sadly failing, she sat in the chair by the fire and received the family, smilingly performing her priestly function by habit. I think, too, of the innumerable near-identical wedding receptions at the Club, where the older ladies command a table next to the dance floor, there offering their blessings to all who will receive.

In these functions, the old uphold a certain respect for ceremony, an important part of life itself. Ceremony imposes a modicum of dignity on our lives, providing cadence and pace to our often hurried or stumbling steps. Most important of all though, it lifts us out of our individual inward-facing selves and makes us part of a community of our fellows. I don't think it's too much to say that as an old man you must be a guardian of ceremony not just for the pleasure it will give you, which is considerable, but for the sake of your family and the community itself.

I've made your role seem extraordinarily passive, as though all you should do is wait in the wings until your presence and blessings are requested. I hope you'll go beyond that and take a lead in preserving tradition. For many years, Josephine and Alden hosted the family's early summer picnic at their lake house, and Colie and Ann the late summer swimming party. And only last year, Alden insisted that the rehearsal dinner before the wedding of his grandson be held at his home, because it was the home of the groom's great-grandfather. Certainly you can do as well.

No Priestly Role for You

Dear Old Man,

I've been thinking lately that in times past you wanted to become a preacher and that some flicker of that desire has never entirely burned out. My recollections began, appropriately enough, on a Sunday morning in church, when I was in the choir as usual, trying in vain to concentrate on the words of the preacher, when my mind wandered off. I faced, at least for a few minutes, the frightening question, "How would God want you to spend what years you have ahead?"

You will remember that for two periods of your life you actually aimed to become a minister. As a boy, saturated with the Baptist tradition, you planned for several years how you would make the ministry your lifework. As a young physician, you dreamed of retiring in your early fifties to go to seminary to become an Episcopal priest. Fortunately, you were saved from both courses, because in each instance your motivation was clearly suspect. But now, nearing sixty-five, might you not still become a minister? Might you do so now for the right rather than the wrong reasons? Might that be God's will?

You didn't think all this out in church that day, for none too soon the sermon ended, and you were singing again, but the question wouldn't leave. The Episcopal seminary at Sewanee isn't far away. Perhaps you could be accepted despite your age. Your summer cottage in Beersheba is barely thirty miles from there. You and Ann could live in Beersheba while you commuted to Sewanee for three years. What better place to live and study, free from the distractions of the world? You have a remarkable capacity for fantasy, and you exercised that faculty to the fullest for several hours before acknowledging the absurdity of it all.

No, you can never become a minister. Neither the Lord nor the church ever chose you for that role. That is but one of your fantasies that you must give up permanently. And a good thing too, because you're not at all suited for the priesthood. The tedium of church meetings would exasperate you; the endless dissatisfactions of the congregation would irritate you beyond measure; the pettiness of church politics would surpass your tolerance. You would quickly become an angry, malcontented minister, burdened by a new load of sins peculiar to the ministry. You are far better off to have finally put that behind you.

You will almost certainly find something that suits you better to put in its place. You will find a ministry of some sort, a good ministry, waiting for you. Even though the time before retirement is short and I still can't foresee exactly what it will be, I am certain you will find a role in service that will need all your energy. Building houses for the poor, feeding the hungry, doing all those pesky and vexacious little jobs needed to keep your church running smoothly – you will fill some need.

For you though, the role must be one of follower rather than of leader, not because you're naturally humble but because you're not a very effective leader. You know how often you've said, in humor yet quite seriously, that you could have been the perfect butler. I hope it doesn't strike you as profane that I imagine your fantasy of being a minister was that you might be chief butler in the house of the Lord, conducting people into and out of His presence, subtly cuing them as to how they should behave there, and always, always, seeing that the service is impeccable. Now you must be willing to be just a footman or a page, always on call for any little job that comes along, moving in and out of the room so stealthily that no one notices.

I grow uneasy when I write you about God's will for you in your old age. I'm so very aware how easy it is to confuse our will for God's will. I recognize now that my penchant to become a minister was solely my will. I pray you don't make that mistake again as you search for a new ministry in your old age.

❧ *The Going Gets Rough*

Dear Old Man,

In my last letters to you I've been dawdling, putting off, hesitant even to set out to deal honestly with you about the most difficult problems of old age – what are you to do when the going really gets rough? Even as I begin this letter, I'm not sure whether my hesitancy arises because I'm so unsure of the answers, or because the answers are so alarming I lack courage to write them down. I suspect the latter.

I've decided to tackle these problems today because of an encounter with a patient earlier this week. His wife, an elderly lady whom I've known for many years, has problems with arthritis, poor vision, and heart failure. She's grown so frail and uncertain in her walking that now she moves slowly and uses a cane. She still has kept her quick and nimble mind, and in her thinking she's adjusted amazingly well to the trials of old age. She's learned well how to deal with an increasingly problem filled life. She came to me with her husband though, asking if anything could be done to help him.

He has always been a strong yet gentle man, successful and widely beloved. With age he's suffered a succession of strokes, leaving his mind in shambles and his gait tottering. Of late, he's begun to hallucinate. In the dead of night he thinks he hears his wife calling, telling him of some danger, and he cries out to her to get the gun so that he can protect them. Sometimes he rises up and falls trying to respond to her imagined call.

Their situation is almost more than his wife can bear, and as she sat talking with me calmly and rationally about their situation, she said, "Oh, Charlie! This life we are leading is terrible, just terrible. All I want now is for it to be over, but the end won't come, and I can't do a thing about it."

They continue to live in the large townhouse where they raised their children. Both of them realize they have become a constant worry if not yet a true burden to their children, who want them to move to a retirement community where housekeeping chores would be fewer and help in an emergency close at hand. But that would mean giving up their home which is a part of their very existence. Now the husband needs full-time nursing help, which would be even more intrusive in a smaller space. Neither of them can contemplate moving him to a nursing home. And so I sat with her and let her tell me of her woe. I just listened, knowing that I have no solutions for these good people, knowing indeed that there are no good solutions.

They must find their way, as I must find mine. What I do know, though, is that I must make my plans now for you, my elder shadow, for eventualities such as these. I must not wait until such problems overwhelm me, until the magnitude of the problems and the frailty of my faculties paralyze me. I must at least set out for myself a plan of action, and I must hope, if the time comes when I need it, that I shall have the strength to put my plan in motion.

What should you do if you find yourself in the position of the husband I've described above? In his old age, he has come close to living up to the tenets I've set out for you, yet he finds himself in a dungeon of life, where all of his choices are bad.

What are your choices? So far as I can see, you have only two: (1) living much as you have been, making whatever cosmetic changes are possible in your support system, hoping to live out your life in your own home; or (2) moving into a nursing home, removing the burden of your daily care from your wife and leaving her the choice of continuing to live at home or move to a more supportive environment.

If you are to live up to the precepts I've set out for you in earlier letters, the choice is clear: you must move to a nursing home. There can be no other choice, at least not with the limited wisdom I now possess. You must insist on moving to a nursing home, and the quicker the better.

The move may come to you as a relief. The concern that I hear most often from my older patients is that they not become a burden to their children. Although it's said less often, an even greater fear must be of becoming a burden to their spouse. I could not bear to see myself become a twenty-four-hour-load to Ann. Moving to a nursing home doesn't remove the burden entirely, but it does exempt her from the physical demands of your daily care. In your condition, that is one of the few things you have left to give.

The other alternative is unacceptable. You must not require of your wife and children the physical and emotional sacrifices required to shepherd you through a long and trying illness at home.

Now you must also ask yourself what you should do if Ann were the more severely incapacitated and if she insisted on moving to a nursing home. You must at least consider this possibility and plan for it, even though you know you will oppose such a move and will fight it with every argument you can muster. You will interpret her insistence, and rightly so, as a statement that her needs are beyond your capacities to provide, and acknowledging your limitations will be painful to you. Moreover, for her to take such a step will bring not only the pain of separation but also the demand of adjusting yourself to a new life almost but not quite alone. But if she insists, you really will have no recourse. She has always been a strong woman, and it is her choice and not yours.

❧ The Last Way Station

Dear Old Man,

If you should go into a nursing home, the last way station in life's journey, how should you deal with your life there? My answer is that you must accept it as the last and most difficult challenge of your life. And while there, you must play the role of "happy camper" to the very end – not only for your family, but for yourself as well – to preserve your own self-esteem and dignity. This will be your ultimate act of love for them and for you.

This is virtually a "Mission Impossible," and as I write I can almost hear the words of that television series beginning, "Your mission, if you choose to accept it, is . . . ." Your mission is to continue to look for good in life, even in such a setting. You must continue to be interested in the world you have left and in the world you have entered. You must give the appearance of having adjusted to the move.

Your world will have contracted, but it will nevertheless be full, and you must concern yourself with it. You have another role to play, but this is nothing new for you. For many years now, the very foundation of your daily life and work has been built on the premise that we can grow to become the roles we act, so you may even find some perverse security in this new role. Can you become the Olivier of the nursing home, playing the benign and not too befuddled older gentleman?

You will take an avuncular interest in the staff, charming

them and making them concerned for you, yet being cautious not to ask too much of them. You will be friendly and concerned with other residents, for you must not hold yourself apart. If you have a telephone, keep in touch with your friends and family. But don't expect many visits except from those who consider it their duty – and remember not to press them for visits, even inadvertently. Continue to read, to listen to the radio, to look at television, for they are your lifelines to the world outside – and they give you something to discuss with your family to convince them that you really aren't doing too badly, that the move to the nursing home was the right choice.

And in the nights, when you are truly alone, what are you to do? First of all, you can pray, and if you can force yourself to pray for others and not focus all the attention on your own needs, so much the better. And you can reminisce. There are many happy times in your life to be relived, and you can experience them again and again in your memory and even displace the present with them. Only last night, when I awoke in the dark hours, I began thinking about when I first went to New York and was a "fair-haired boy," one of the chosen few. Though the memory was saddened by the thought that none of that dear tribe is any longer a "fair-haired boy," it was, even so, a delicious memory. And there are a host like them. Night can also be a time for fantasy, for dreaming once more all those daydreams of youth, when all was possible, when all doors were open, when all you had to do was close your eyes to find yourself in a magic land.

Night offers so many opportunities that it may well become your favorite time, a time when you can wrap yourself in a warm aloneness and isolation and privacy. This can be your time for work, because there is still plenty of work to be done. You've got to come to terms with your life, balance your books, put behind you if you can all the wrongs you've committed – perhaps even harder, put to rest the hopeless dreams of all that you wanted so badly but haven't been able to accomplish. You must work at forgiving, both yourself and others. You mustn't fall into the habit of totting up only your debits, because you have credits too, and they deserve your attention. My prayer for you now is that in this summing up, you will come to believe that you have done pretty well with the talents and weaknesses you were given – that you have at least come close to fulfilling your potential.

Night can also be a time for planning your days. By now you almost certainly won't be able to see ahead more than one day at a time. I already know what your biggest problem on that next day will be – controlling your temper. You have always been quick to anger, and on occasions your anger has exploded into rage, almost always in situations where you have felt powerless. Life in the nursing home will be made up of a parade of irritating occurrences, varying mainly in their magnitude; in almost every one you will be powerless. In fact, not since infancy will you have felt so powerless, and the only way you may gain any measure of control over a situation will be by guile, not by strength. So you must plot your days with care. You can retain some control over your daily life, but only if your anger and rage are well hidden, if they serve only as fuel for your cunning and craftiness.

Still, you must not consume your precious night hours

thinking only of yourself; you must continue to think of others, even if the others you can touch have dwindled to just a few family members and those in your nursing home. You can still do good, by word if not by deed, but in order to do so, you must accomplish a difficult task – maintain your giving spirit. You will need to plan your good deeds carefully, perhaps even force yourself to do them, whereas, in earlier years, they may have come without thought or even awareness. You must, nevertheless, find some way to keep this part of you living.

❦ At Home on Your Own

Dear Old Man,

It will be much more difficult for you if your roles are reversed – if Ann should decide to enter a nursing home and leave you at home on your own. Your house or apartment will no longer be home without her there, and certainly her room in the nursing home can never be home to you. What role can I create for you who have always been most comfortable being a host, never so much being a guest?

Clearly, if it's at all possible, you must maintain your home, and by "maintain," I mean keep it lovingly. Fortunately, this will require a considerable amount of your time and effort, since you and Ann have always loved beautiful objects in beautiful surroundings. In anticipation of any visits she might make home, you must keep the place as bright and burnished as if she were still living there. Beyond that, though, it would make her unhappy to think of you living in some makeshift place, for her decision to go into the nursing home was dictated more by her perception of your needs than by her own.

That will be the easy part of the job. You've never had any problem being a househusband. It will be much harder for you to continue your life in the community without her at your side, but that is exactly what you must do. In large part, she decided upon the nursing home so that you wouldn't give up your life to be a full-time nurse. You must accept this generous gift from her, but it won't be easy – you've also been much better at giving than at receiving. Thus, even in your loneliness, you will continue to go to church, to parties, to community activities, to movies, to weddings, to family celebrations, even though most probably you would rather be sitting at her side. This may be even tougher to deal with than her death, because she is still there, and all around will be the recurrent question, "How's Ann getting along?" In these musings I'm beginning to have more understanding and sympathy for Wesley, who gave up everything to stay with his invalid wife. Perhaps he did so simply because he'd rather be at her side than anywhere else, perhaps because he couldn't bear to squander even one hour on things less valuable.

In all these outside activities, you must walk a narrow path. Whatever you may feel, you must appear neither too sad nor too glad. You must avoid being morose out of deference to Ann and her friends. At the same time you must be cheerful, but not too cheerful. No one should have cause to say, "He looks as though he doesn't have a care in the world, and Ann still in a nursing home!" Fortunately, most of the time your mind will be on your job, which will be to listen and report. Ann has always brought the real world home to you in her nightly account of friends and community; she has always amused and diverted you from the narrowness of your daily life, thereby enriching you immeasurably. Now the roles are reversed. Wherever you go, you will search for little stories to pass along to her. Almost nothing is too small. Remember the young woman who greeted you at the plant store yesterday, asking if the white anemones she'd found for you last fall had survived the winter, and they had. Ann's so often remarked, "All the women in the plant stores know you." This will certainly amuse her.

You must, of course, do more than just go through the motions of living so that you can amuse Ann with anecdotes. By choosing to enter the nursing home, she gave you a generous gift. But the gift carries with it responsibilities – you must truly learn to live a portion of your life on your own without her, to live a life apart from her. I pray you will be equal to the challenge.

❧ Money Matters

Dear Old Man,

Money matters! Give it attention. Indeed, treat it as a subject of vital importance, for in old age and often earlier in life it can be a recurring source of conflict between the generations. In no other area is it so important for you to think clearly, act decisively, and communicate clearly to your heirs.

A fundamental question must be answered first. To whom do your assets belong? Or to put the question more exactly, to whom do you assign your assets? Once you answer that question, the answer to many others follows easily. The question has the potential for conflict in almost every family, though it is almost never openly confronted. It is clearly in the parents' best interest that the assets be assigned to them, and it is clearly in the children's best interest that the assets be assigned to the family collectively.

The origins of these conflicts lie not only in under-standable human want and need but in history. Primogen-iture, for example, asserted the importance of family, even if only of one family member, over the individual. On the other hand, my own father would have had good cause to believe, though I have no evidence that he ever did, that a portion of his father's wealth rightly belonged to him indi-vidually, because he had worked hard in his youth to help raise the family out of its relative poverty. And since your sons and daughter know that you inherited property from your parents, they must certainly question whether this was a personal or a family legacy.

I believe it is best for you to make it quite clear that whatever wealth you may possess in your old age will serve to support you and Ann, in whatever style you choose and can afford, during your lives, and that any remainder will be divided equally among your sons and daughter. Your initial reponse will probably be, "But Charles, that is obvious." It may be obvious to you, but it's often not explicated and understood. Ownership must be acknowledged and asserted, else you will be prey to guilt for every dollar spent that might "go to the children," or they will resent you for spending *their* inheritance. In this, I insist that you don't owe your children anything, just as in another letter I have insisted that they don't owe you anything for having conceived and nurtured them.

I am not suggesting you should not be generous to your children if your financial position allows it. On the contrary, I hope you will be, but I also hope the impulse will arise out of generosity and genuine love for them, not out of some misguided sense of duty. Even generosity and love can prove risky if you are not careful. You must never use them to exert power over your sons and daughter. This happens most easily when money fosters dependency. You will recall Mrs. Grant, whose children are now well over fifty. Throughout their adult lives, she has supported them with her wealth so that their families might live in a style far above that which her sons could support on their earnings. Mrs. Grant is a generous woman, and I am convinced that she has done this with the best of motives, but she has thereby created families who are utterly dependent on her; they must come to her for every significant need. If she wished to provide them the luxuries in life, she should have turned over to them, perhaps in trusts, sizable portions of her wealth when they were young, so that they could have learned to manage the income, whether well or not. Instead, she has remained the fountain of wealth and largesse to whom they must turn for everything beyond the essentials in life. So far as I know, she always gives them whatever they ask for, whether it be a cruise for the family to the Arctic Circle, or tuition for a grandson's graduate school education, and she gives joyfully. But her children remain dependent, little motivated to achieve, and totally ignorant of how to manage money – and the money will almost certainly run out long before they die. Poor rich Mrs. Grant's only legacy in the long run will be their memories of her generosity and of luxuries now beyond their grasp.

The other pitfall you must avoid is using money to buy favors under the guise of making a gift. Let me make myself clear. I don't think there is anything wrong with buying favors so long as it's clear and above board. For example, I think it's fine to say to a son, "We'd be glad to pay all the expenses for two weeks in the mountains next summer *if* you and your family are willing to come stay with us," or to propose paying private school tuition for a grandchild *if* that grandchild is willing to maintain a passing average. Problems will inevitably arise, though, if you are in fact not making a gift but are surreptitiously bargaining for something else, especially if your object is unacknowledged and is to be gained at some unspecified time in the future. Parents often try to use gifts to their children in early years to buy care for themselves in old age, a practice to be condemned unless the strings attached to the gifts are made clear. For example, it's fine for grandparents to help in the daily care of their grandchildren, either because they want to be helpful or simply for the joy it provides. It's not acceptable, though, if the grandparent secretly expects to be *repaid* later, when that help is no longer needed, with comparable time and attention from their children. Another example is assisting a son or daughter to buy a house larger than their family really needs with the secret hope of being asked to move in if disability strikes. You must learn to expect nothing in return for gifts, to expect full compliance with *quid pro quo* agreements.

As you grow old, you may perceive the need not only for someone to care for you physically but also for someone to look after your everyday financial affairs such as depositing checks and paying bills. Only if there is absolutely no one else available should you turn to your sons or daughter for this assistance. Unless you limit yourself to a modest and simple existence, they cannot, unless they have truly generous dispositions, avoid looking upon each expenditure as a subtraction, and often an unwarranted one at that, from their inheritance that you must justify to them.

Never, never give over to your children all your assets, even if it is firmly agreed that they will turn over the income from those assets, or even the principal if need be, for your care until your death. That would put you in the uneasy position of having to ask them for everything you need or want; it puts them in nearly as bad a position, having to give permission for everything you spend. Perhaps more important, money is power. At a time in life when your power is dribbling away, you need to hold on to as much of it as you can – so that you can at least appear gracious and accepting about the power you can't keep from losing. Holding on to control over your financial affairs carries with it responsibilities that you must be willing to shoulder. You must keep close tab on your assets, use or invest them prudently, and get good financial advice. If you insist on maintaining control, you have a responsibility to continue your interest.

Last, I must give you some advice about a situation that I hope doesn't arise, which is if Ann should die first and you should later choose to remarry. Financial problems in this situation are almost inevitable, and they give rise to some of the bitterest and most unyielding family squabbles. If you find yourself contemplating a second marriage, you should first take steps to assure that any assets you have inherited from Ann are taken out of your estate and put into trust for your children, so that there is no possibility that any of her capital will be diverted to your second wife. Next, you and your wife-to-be must execute a prenuptial financial agreement to assure that if she survives you, the principal of your estate will eventually go only to your children, though providing for her continuing needs from income if she has need of it. If your wife-to-be has children of her own, her assets should be similarly protected for her children. Never make the mistake of entering a second marriage without spelling out the financial arrangements openly and in detail beforehand.

✒ Dear God in Heaven

Dear Old Man,

I couldn't write this letter to anyone but you. I've always been such a private person – Ann calls me taciturn – especially so about matters of faith. Nevertheless, I can't advise you how to grow old and leave out something so vital to your daily life. I'm writing about prayer, which can become the chief sustaining force in your daily life, as you with God's help finally mature. I'm speaking of course of your private prayer, that time you allot each day to the intimate company of God.

As you well know, I'm no expert on prayer. All I can possibly tell you is my personal idea of how you might expand this experience in the years ahead. Your own habits of prayer have been inconsistent over the years. In childhood you prayed compulsively, your prayers then little more than a wish list you presented each day to the giver of all good gifts, along with fervent supplications that He protect you from the sins you were committing each day. In youth and young manhood, you never ceased to pray, but the habit of prayer slipped away, giving way to brief exclamations begging protection in one or another crisis of the moment.

As you have grown older, though, your prayer life has changed and grown, even though it's still no better than a puny plant in need of constant coddling. It has, nevertheless, become a more constant habit, one you turn to almost every day, so that without it your day is incomplete. Your daily prayers have grown longer, and you've begun at last to pray more for the needs of others than for your own, though this may be but the result of how wonderfully blessed you have been. Even so, this part of your life has plenty of room for healthy growth and pruning as well. Old age may be the ideal time to take on this task.

First of all, you must cordon off a segment of time each day and devote it, uninterrupted, to prayer. You know how your praying has been piggybacked onto daily activities that require little thought, as you've found time for prayer while driving back and forth to work, walking, exercising on the Nordic Track – almost any time in fact except those of quiet and isolation. You must remedy this, because true prayer requires every bit of attention you can muster.

You've heard it said that, "You'd better be careful what you pray for, because it might be given to you." Maybe that's been in the back of my mind, for many of my petitions have been uttered with unspoken reservations. I may pray, "Help me to become . . . . . " but hope not too soon. Or, "Help me to do thy will . . . ." but hope His will agrees with mine. This has struck me recently as I've begun to think and pray about retirement. What if it is the Lord's will that I continue working as a physician instead of retiring and turning to something new? Can I unreservedly pray that His will and not mine be done?

As you carve out more time for prayer, you've got to change the way you pray as well. Most of your prayers, if overheard, would probably sound like a grant request to the Almighty – a one way wireless communication across time and space, begging mostly for miracles. You've never given

God enough time to answer back – certainly you've not taken enough time to perceive the Holy Spirit working in you. So you must change your prayer time from talking to God more to listening for God. You must spend your time truly waiting upon the Lord.

All this sounds like a big order for an old man. On the other hand, it's something you couldn't have achieved as a younger one. You might even think of it as a task God has saved especially for your old age – a task in which age is a helper and not an impediment. There is still time enough to do it right.

❧ Curious, and Still Learning

Dear Old Man,

Last week I read a piece by Robertson Davies in the *Times Book Review*[1] in which he said, "Curiosity, it appears to me, is the greatest preservative and the supreme emollient . . . . curiosity about something. Enthusiasm. Zest. That's what makes old age . . . a delight."

I had planned to write that you must keep yourself "interested" in something, but I like his word "curious" much better, as it brings a greater sense of action, of adventure. One can be passively interested, but it's difficult to think of anyone being passively curious.

Having written this, I recognize that it violates one of my rules of "advice giving," which is that one should never tell a person to *be* something he isn't, for that may well exceed his capacities. The most one should ask is that someone act in a certain way. Indeed, in the same essay Davies points out: "What ails most [old people], and what has ailed them all their lives, is that they lack curiosity. They have never engaged themselves strongly in anything. The waters of life have washed over them without anything soaking in."

So I shall tell you only to *act* interested, to *act* curious about something. If this strikes you as mechanistic or

1. Robertson Davies, "You're Not Getting Older, You're Getting Nosier," *The New York Times Book Review*, 12 May 1991.

phony, I make no apologies, but I urge this on you only as a beginning. It's truly difficult to *be* interested in a topic you know little about. Begin by casting about for something that might interest you, then learn about it and see if it doesn't lead you into the wonderland of true curiosity. I will go a step further, though, and suggest that if you are looking around for something to interest yourself in, consider something of special and current interest to the young.

On the other hand, there's certainly nothing wrong with devoting yourself to something obscure that catches the eye of no one else you know. My mind is flooded with recollections of my friends who have developed true curiosity. Marc collects books by a single author, and as his bibliophilic tastes are satisfied, he comes to know the author and the author's world. Billy began to learn Chinese and in his solitary way even tried his hand at calligraphy. Mr. Wills began to grow iris and became a renowned hybridizer. Ann started to collect maps and over the years grew into a scholar of their genealogy. Whatever the object of your interest, you will learn, and that is probably the true objective. For the essence of being alive is learning.

I am diverted by that last phrase, which raises in my mind the distinction between "living" and "being alive." Obviously, one can live – and probably the vast majority of people do – through life without ever being alive. One cannot, however, imagine a person's being alive who lacks the curiosity that leads to growth. Curiosity may, of course, be tightly focused: a pianist might easily spend a lifetime seeking to perfect his performance of Schubert's *Impromptus*. In that case, danger lies in wait, for almost certainly the nearer one grows to perfection, the more likely it is that curiosity will dissipate into mere repetitiveness. I think of the banality of much of Picasso's later work. I think also of Yul Brynner, who must have spent thirty years or more playing the role of the King of Siam, many thought to perfection. Yet the story is told that wherever he travelled with the show over the years, he required his bedroom to be painted dark brown. From this bit of trivia, I suspect that rather than growing in the role of the king, Brynner achieved only a sameness in each performance, which, though extremely polished and exciting for the audience, was nothing more to him than another night's work.

Thoughts about being alive arouse questions about whom one is alive for – for oneself or for others. You will recall one of your friends who carries fascination with her ancestors to the level of worship. There is no question that she is vitally alive to herself, but to others she is dead. Not only that, her friends feel their thoughts congealing whenever she begins to talk about her mostly undistinguished forebears who appear to be what she values most in life. If at your age you have the luxury to choose an interest, fix on something if you can that interests others, especially the young, as well as yourself. Otherwise, acknowledge openly the oddity of your special interests, laugh at yourself for them, and make certain you don't bore others talking about them.

I recall for you the dinner you had with Chancellor Branscomb, now ninety-six years of age, a vestige of his former physical self, but with brainpower undiminished.

He lamented, but without self pity, that he can no longer see to read, "but," he said, "I can still write." He went on to say that he now spends time composing poems or limericks in his mind, then writing them down. He talked of this with spirit and recited one or two for us. Recently, he said, Mrs. Branscomb had had a birthday. When he asked what she wanted from him as a present, she asked only for "a poem." What else is there to say on this topic?

I Must Give You Strength

Dear Old Man,

As I continue my one-sided correspondence with you, I begin to feel more and more that I am a nag and a scold, always chiding and filling the air with "do this" and "don't do that." I hear myself sounding like a hypercritical parent who will just never shut up. I grow heavy and ponderous with you, self-righteous in my tone, and I wonder that you can read even one more suggestion or admonition from such a humorless correspondent. If I were you, I would probably stop reading these tiresome and unamusing missives. But then I *am* you and must force myself to think these troublesome thoughts and to put them down for you.

I gave a few of these letters to my friend Bill Petrie, himself an expert on old age, asking ostensibly if they ring true but really asking, of course, for his approval. His first comment to me was, "They're so depressing I can hardly read them! Can't you find something bright to say about growing old?" He's right, of course, in addition to being an optimist, for in truth I don't find much to look forward to in old age. This is probably a pattern I've followed all my life. I've always aimed to prepare myself for the worst, hoping to be pleasantly surprised when a situation turned out not so bad as anticipated.

I can't help wondering if I'll ever read these letters when they are really needed, wondering if I'll even be able to read them or to hear them read to me. And if I can't, will I really care? Might I not just feel relieved?

How can I force myself to continue to care? Is there somewhere a hidden source of strength to sustain not just the hope to endure old age with grace but also to become someone better? For most certainly there will be other voices whispering messages of resignation, beckoning you to give up, take the easy way out, cease the struggle. They will tempt by telling you that you have run your race and deserve whatever years of ease and rest may be left to you. And you will listen oh so longingly and want oh so much to give yourself up to these cloying counsels.

Somehow through these letters I must give you strength not to die in the midst of life, even if you are old. How many people can you now recall who died as persons even in their forties and fifties, yet lived on year after year as empty shells, less alive than the shadows of living people? Certainly you remember the Greens, who lived out their days in luxury but whose minds never ventured further than to wonder when they might have that first drink of the day or to talk of the everyday life of their everyday friends. They were not bad people, mind you, just lifeless.

You must heed what I write and not let that happen to you. You will recall a study done many years ago of Peace Corps volunteers that showed success in their missions to correlate only with the precision and exactness with which they had planned their future lives. If I can prod you now to chart your course clearly, you just may reach your objective.

ᕈ Friendships Attain an Intimacy

Dear Old Man,

Aside from good health and a caring family, friendships are probably the most valuable assets a person can carry into old age. For many years I believed that close and intimate friendships seldom develop once we are past our twenties. This was a view from the broad plains of my middle years, before I looked toward the crags of old age. I now believe that friendships attain their full richness only in old age, and those who die young never know the fullness that friendship can attain in life's last years.

In middle age, friendships may be sustained or wither, but they seldom grow, for most of one's energy is poured into family and work, and little remains even for sustaining a friendship. Not that it takes much effort really. Clyde Ryals, now a distinguished Victorian scholar at Duke University, and a friend of almost fifty years, and I have not lived in the same community for well over forty years, but we seldom fail to telephone on the other's birthday. We rarely communicate otherwise, but that is enough to keep our friendship alive and even healthy. When we did manage to get together for dinner this past summer, once again we found that the years had not broken any of the ties of our affection.

More often the middle years are those when friendships falter, either through neglect or through some slighting or hurtful act. Ann has remarked to me that if we broke off with all of our friends who at one time or time have given us some offense, we might find ourselves reaching old age with no friends at all. I think now of the Glasses, with whom we had shared a table at a charity event for many years. When I called at one point to confirm the arrangement for that year, the husband told me that they'd been asked to sit with a prominent out-of-town businessman, and thus could not join us. This was a cut which bothered us for some time, yet we've gone on being friends, and in recent years our friendship has once again flourished. Another friend, repeatedly tactless and thoughtlessly critical in her conversation, shows her love for us and for others through her actions, and we smile through her words. I realize that sadly enough I have probably been equally and unwittingly insensitive with other good friends and have given them justification for breaking with me. I am grateful they haven't. Thus the middle years often require an abundance of patience and tolerance and forgiving for friendships to survive. We must, nevertheless, make sure they survive, for it would be tragic to arrive at the portals of old age without a host of friends at our side.

It seems to me that in old age friendships often attain an intimacy of affection, though possibly not of self-revelation, seldom reached in youth. It is as though each loss from the group through death or confinement binds the survivors together even more closely. It appears to me, too, that older friends are often more tolerant and accepting than younger ones. Older friends frequently criticize each other and argue with a bluntness that would have cleaved ties in earlier years, yet the hostility has been distilled out of the words so that no umbrage is taken.

Older friends are also often more tolerant and accepting of their friends' failings and limitations than are those who are more youthful. For example, one of my step-mother's friends, all of whom are now in their eighties, has fairly advanced Alzheimer's Disease; even so, they manage to include her in almost all their activities. I think too of an elderly friend who has severe loss of short-term memory, so that she can recall little of what happened yesterday or even five minutes ago. Yet her friends regularly take her with them for dinner, to parties and concerts, to meetings – all of which she appears to enjoy enormously though she cannot recall them even a few hours later. Friends in old age have the capacity for burying the enmities that divided them in the past and living for the present. A mellowing occurs between them that is seldom evident earlier. It is as though love and affection carry the day, whatever may have happened in the past.

If you think about it a bit, I believe you'll agree with me that in old age, friends are the only ones who accept you and love you *just* the way you are, not paying much attention to your failings or feeling the need to improve or better you. Children, and perhaps even your spouse, will love you *despite* the way you are, *despite* all your failings. You will recall that your father-in-law was blessed in his last years with many friends who overlooked his failing memory and enjoyed him for his wit and enthusiasms. One of his friends for many years was Dr. Henry Hill, the retired President of

Peabody College. Both were then widowers, and every Saturday night they joined the same group of friends for dinner at their club. Dr. Hill had given up driving because of poor vision, but Colie continued to drive despite increasing confusion and the admonitions of his daughters. He and Dr. Hill were a great pair in their social activities though, for as Dr. Hill put it, "Colie can still see to drive, and I can still remember how to find the way to where we're going."

In your old age, I suspect it will be only your friends who can give to you unreservedly. Recall again, if you will, how Colie's friends in the apartment building banded together to help keep him living independently despite his gradual descent into dementia. Somehow friends were always at his side to guide him through the maze his days had become. I believe friends are able to do this because they are able to love fully and to help each other without feeling truly responsible for each other. Blood ties knot us in bonds of responsibility. Thus with family members, issues of power and a true sense of responsibility always arise. Only friends can be unreservedly giving.

And finally, it will be your friends who mourn you unreservedly at your death and help you or Ann mourn the other. With children, feelings of loss are almost always tempered by a sense of relief from worry and responsibility, and, especially when there is a significant amount of money or property involved, by a sense of comfort that cannot be entirely put to flight by guilt.

You will recall that one of my finest memories of friendship in old age is of a little incident that occurred after Vernon Sharp's funeral. After the conclusion of the services at the grave, Ellen Wills insisted on riding back with Sarah Sharp to her country house, her first journey home after Vernon's death. I will always cherish the image of these two old ladies, friends for more than sixty years and now both widows, sitting alone in the back seat of the car, Ellen holding Sarah's hands in her own and saying, "We'll just go back to Inglehame together."

⤖ Is There No Rest for the Weary?

Dear Old Man,

As I read back over these letters and think about their message, I'm struck again and again by how much I am asking of you as an old man. In many ways I'm asking of you more wisdom, more strength, and more determination than you've been able to summon up in your earlier years. In fact, I know that I'm asking more than you can ever give. Why am I doing this? Am I just setting you up for failure at a time in life when you can least suffer it?

I don't have the answer, of course, but in a series of letters filled to overflowing with "should's" and "ought's" and "must's," I at least ought to acknowledge to you a few of my doubts. There is no question that I've asked of you an old age of endurance, of self-denial, of continuing struggle, a life in which reason, right, and the needs of others almost always prevail, a life in which wishes, wants, feelings, and pleasures are nearly always subordinated. Is there truly to be no rest for the weary?

For me even to ask such a question comes as a surprise. So far I've written these letters with what is for me unusual assurance, a sure sense that I was delineating for you the finest way to grow old. Yet I can take a different look and be highly critical. "It seems to me, Charles, that you're always trying to make a virtue out of doing whatever is difficult or distasteful." "Charles, aren't you making old age as driven as you have the rest of your life, out of some misbegotten belief that life should be built up of acts you don't want to do, done out of a sense of duty or responsibility or guilt – that only in this does true virtue lie?"

No question that is part of my makeup. The strict fundamentalism in which I was reared still speaks in the voice of my conscience. Hard work is the highest virtue, and hard work is supposed to be hard. If it is a joy or pleasure, how can it be work? Only a little less virtuous are "good works," which consist almost entirely of doing those things one really doesn't want to do. Although when I was a child in church, we often sang "Amazing Grace," in our lives grace was given only token respect, for salvation clearly lay in hard work and good works. Salvation had to be *earned,* and earned the hard way.

I tell myself, of course, that I've outgrown this, or that I've transformed those beliefs into something quite different. And to a certain extent that's true. I know, though, that they still lurk inside me, ready to reassert themselves at the least opportunity. I tell myself that each of us has some capacity for heroism, and that my highest aim should be to live up to that potential, even if I am the only one to know I have reached that goal. Obviously, heroism never comes easily. It's not heroic if it's not sacrificial.

Perhaps I missed my cue, if I missed it at all, in failing to recognize that a hero's life isn't made up solely of heroic acts. Heroes don't have to act heroically for always and forever. Indeed, proud countries often crown their heroes with a life of leisure, witness Marlborough and Blenheim Palace. "You have done enough, no more is required." Was Lindbergh's fatal flaw that he could not rest the hero but had to keep proving over and over that he really was a hero? Not that I compare myself with Lindbergh, of course, except in my belief that each of us has some capacity for acts that push us, perhaps for ever so brief a time, into a level of existence beyond that of our ordinary lives, when what we do is touched ever so slightly by the divine. In those moments we recognize that we are living not for ourselves alone, but for some greater good beyond our human understanding.

It may surprise your daughter and sons to learn that their father, who in every respect appears so ordinary and conventional, harbors such fantasies. Yet they probably guessed it, if in no other way than from your repeated viewing of *Chariots of Fire.* You will recall that in the movie Abrahams and Liddell won Olympic gold medals and became heroes to the nation. On the other hand, Aubrey, as a man, was a hero and their equal, even though he won no medals at all. Aubrey perceived himself accurately as a perfectly ordinary human being, but he pushed himself to become something more, and became, along with Abrahams and Liddell, a part of something larger than himself. And then they – all of them – rested.

That is my valedictory to you. Yes, in these letters I often call on you for sacrifice, if you will, for a heroism that will be known only to you. But I don't demand of you heroism in every situation, and I beg that you not ask of yourself more than you can give. Continue to strive, but make of your life something more than just striving. You are an old man now. You have lived honorably even if far from perfectly. It's all right now to rest a little.

❧ An Old Man's Best Friend

Dear Old Man,

Do not go gentle into that good night without your dog beside you. A few years ago, such a statement would have struck you as the height of silliness or perhaps a failed effort at humor. That was, of course, before Ramona came into your life and changed it forever.

I still don't understand the intense longing for a dog of your very own that arose in you a few years ago, a longing neither you nor anyone who knew you could have predicted. It was likely the remnant of some childhood dream, forgotten but never completely erased. As a boy, you'd asked for a dog, perhaps because you thought it was expected of you, and once your father did bring home for you a bright, frisky little puppy. He was soon gone, however, even before you had time to name him, after he threw up all over the back seat of your father's new automobile during your first Sunday afternoon drive. I don't recall feeling bereft or even deprived, but your memory may be even clearer now than mine. Almost certainly you didn't press for another puppy, for your indulgent parents would probably have supplied it.

Clearly though, some spark of desire smouldered on, because soon after you and Ann were married, you bought her a dachshund pup, which you named Bonnie to rhyme with the name of her parents' dog, Honey. Then followed Roly Poly, another dachshund, and Frisky, a black Labrador retriever, which stayed at the side of your sons and daughter until they were away in college. These dogs owed their allegiance though to Ann and the children and not to you. When Frisky died at the age of twelve, you and Ann agreed that life without a dog wasn't necessarily bad, especially as one grows older.

Even so, some gnawing yen must have lingered, because, several years ago, with no apparent cause, you began to talk to Ann about getting a dog – someday. Some months later, you bought a large illustrated book describing the different breeds of dogs, and, after much deliberation, announced that a West Highland white terrier was your choice. Still, several months passed before you actually set out to buy a puppy. You considered only the two females from her litter. Both were funny looking, straggly-haired little creatures, bearing few hints of the beauty that was to come. But when you knelt down to greet them property and called for Ramona, for you had already decided on her name, one waddled over and began licking and nibbling at your fingers. You knew then that she was Ramona, and that she had chosen you.

You, my friend, and I had never before had a dog of our very own. Was I too old to adjust to having a new member of the family? Was I energetic enough to be able to care for her properly? Was I perhaps temperamentally unsuited for this new role as master to a young puppy? The answer to all three questions must have been "no," for she and I have accommodated nicely to life together.

She has brought me delight such as I had thought I would not find again in this life. She has made me feel like a boy again. Each morning when I wake her from sleep in her little house where she is so secure, she comes to me with a trust so certain it is almost palpable. Each evening when I return from work, I hear her little squeals of delight before I can even open the garage door, and she greets me with a boundless joy that humans can almost never show. And in the evening too she brings me peace as she lies sleeping in my lap while I read.

Ramona isn't perfect, of course, either in her behavior or in her conformation. She's spoiled beyond measure, and she wants too much attention and can be annoyingly persistent about getting it. She can be distressingly stubborn too, and at times she pouts. She has a brown spot on her tail, and her ears don't stand up as perkily as should those of a champion of her breed. On the other hand, she's endlessly playful, full of good humor, and she makes us laugh. Is it any wonder I find her perfect?

No, old man, you must never again be without a dog of your very own. If you and Ramona are both lucky, she may outlive you, but if she should die first, even as you grieve you must go out and find yourself another dog. Nothing else can make you feel like a boy again whatever your age – and nothing else can keep you feeling that way simply by its presence.

❧ Keep Dreaming!

Dear Old Man,

Try not to grieve for the dreams you've not lived. Instead thank God that you were able to dream. Thank Him too that you've been able to put so many of those dreams away, not for another day, but forever.

You know that like Walter Mitty I've always lived a life vivid in fantasy. Even though I'm a psychiatrist, I've never been sure whether or not most people turn regularly to such an entertaining life of the imagination, though certainly many do. In some ways it's a wonderful device for coping with the burdens of life, giving one the capacity at almost any time to turn away from boredom or worry to enter a fantasied world where success is sure and failure unknown.

As a young child, I dreamed of being the lost prince who would one day be found, recognized, and presented in robes of court to his parents. This dream may have been born because my parents treated me, an only child, much like a prince. I was smart enough to know that I never had and never would have realms to rule, but that didn't keep me from cherishing this dream. In retrospect, I think I probably put this fantasy away very early not because the chances for its coming true were so slim but because I could never figure out where this would leave my parents, whom I loved dearly.

Later I dreamed of becoming a great pianist, performing all the standard concerti with the great orchestras of the world, to wild applause and adulation. Since my natural talent as a pianist was decidedly slim, I intended to achieve this success through constant practice. And practice I did, for hours on end, day after day. How my parents tolerated this noisy and seemingly tireless compulsion, I'll never know. Fortunately with time, reason prevailed, and while still young, I learned one of life's most valuable lessons – that one cannot achieve every aim through effort alone.

Later, as a college student, I thought of becoming an ambassador, living in colorful capital cities, speaking even obscure languages with ease, and doing I had no idea what. Though my lack of fortune would normally close doors to the posts in London and Paris, even there, I knew a way might be found. Fortunately, when I graduated from college, I was too young to apply for the Foreign Service, for they just might have taken me. Time has shown me to be quite unsuited for a peripatetic life, and I would have lived forever homesick for the home I could never have.

I write not to tell you not to dream but to tell you instead to dream even dreams you know cannot come true. Though none of my patients has ever told me explicitly, I suspect that dreaming can be one of the soothing balms of later life. No matter that doors to action are closed, in dreams one can still walk straight through. In dreams, one can fill a lonely world with special friends of one's very own choosing. In dreams one can leave an ever shrinking world and travel over the earth or even to the stars.

No, do not grieve for the dreams you've not lived. Keep dreaming! Don't let old age rob you of this magical gift.

❧ Let Us Begin

Dear Old Man,

This will be my last letter to you. It's been two and a half years since I wrote the first, and it's time to bring them to a close. It's also time to look for the thread that ties these letters together. I believe that thread is found in my repeated focus on the potential for personal change in older years.

My friend Marc Hollender and I have argued about the nature of old age. Specifically, he has been critical of my view that it is a period of growth and development, for he believes it to be one only of regression and loss. As I think about it, possibly it is my metaphor of growth that he finds most troubling. In my mind, perhaps one can conceive old age best as a time when everything on the outside is withering while everything inside is being distilled to its essence, whether that essence be sweet or bitter. I believe each of us has some choice as to how that essence will taste.

I cannot, of course, prove him wrong; much that we know from experience and observation supports his argument. Old age is unquestionably a time of loss – of faculties, of strength and agility, of beauty, of skills and abilities, of health, of kin and friends, of financial resources, of independence. The list seems endless, and most of my letters to you have concerned how best to deal with one or another of these losses. Even so, I am unwilling to concede that old age must necessarily be marked only by regression, though in fact it may be that for many persons.

I continue to believe that, unless our brains falter seriously, we are capable of growth *as persons* throughout our life span. In old age, we can grow not in stature but in spirit – in tolerance, understanding, modesty, compassion, self-denial, self-awareness, concern for others, generosity, love. And that's what these letters are all about – to stimulate you to keep growing, to keep trying to become a better person than you are.

Frankly, I'm worn out with giving advice – something Ann and our sons and daughter will have trouble believing – and I've come close to exhausting my subject. Even so, I'll miss my correspondence with you. Writing these letters has been a fine experience for me, almost a therapeutic experience, for as I've written you day after day, you've become almost another person to me. As we have talked back and forth, I've come to like you, to care about you, maybe even to love you. Certainly you know this hasn't always been the case; for many years, I've tended to ponder more my faults and shortcomings than what is good in me. All appearances to the contrary, I've not liked myself very much. But in writing these letters, I've been forced to look inward, to peer into corners of my being that I've neglected, perhaps never ever seen. In this probing, I've been surprised to find more girders of strength, more beacons of concern, more filaments of tenderness than I ever dreamed were there. And I've come to like you – a surprise, indeed almost a revelation to me.

Not that I shall ever become the person I've been advising you to become; that's too much to ask either of me or of you. I know though that I shall be trying to become that person, and I shall try not to ask anything more of you than your truest efforts. I shall try to look on that which is good in me rather than stare into the chasm which separates me from perfection.

I hope that Ann and our sons and daughter will be gentle and forgiving when you falter, but, at the same time, that they won't let you slip by without making your best efforts. I know that you'll need both their support and their prodding – indeed their prayers – if you're to achieve your goal and mine.

Since I began these letters to you, old age is no longer on the horizon. It's just a few yards away. The years of preparation are over. It's time for you to begin to practice what I preach. Let us begin, with God's help.

Your friend,
Charles

COLOPHON

This book was composed in Adobe Garamond, a type
face modeled after the designs of Claude Garamond, a
fifteenth-century printer. This version retains most of the
traditional letterforms, and adapts itself well to the digi-
tal process. The book design is the work of Gary Gore.